Bitten by Witch Fever

For Julie, who appreciates the beautiful and the unusual.

Front and back cover wallpaper design by
Corbière, Son & Brindle, London, UK, 1877

Lucinda Hawksley is a Pre-Raphaelite and Aestheticism expert who writes
about social history, literature and the life and works of her great
great great grandfather Charles Dickens. As well as being the author
of more than twenty books, she is an internationally established
television and radio broadcaster. She has lectured at London's
National Portrait Gallery, the William Morris Gallery,
The William Morris Society and the Pre-Raphaelite Society.

First published in the United Kingdom in 2016 by
Thames & Hudson Ltd, 181A High Holborn, London WC1V 7QX

First published in 2016 in hardcover in the
United States of America by Thames & Hudson Ltd,
500 Fifth Avenue, New York, New York 10110

Reprinted 2021

Published in association with The National Archives

The National Archives is the UK government's official archive
containing over 1,000 years of history. They give detailed guidance
to government departments and the public sector on information
management, and advise others about the care of historial archives.

www.nationalarchives.gov.uk

British Library Cataloguing-in-Publication Data
A catalogue record for this book is available from the British Library

Library of Congress Catalog Card Number 2016931246

ISBN 978-0-500-51838-0

Printed and bound in China by Everbest Printing Co. Ltd

MIX
From responsible
sources
FSC® C124385

Lucinda Hawksley

BITTEN BY WITCH FEVER

Wallpaper & Arsenic in the Victorian Home

with over 450 illustrations

Thames&Hudson

The National Archives

TEXTS

INTRODUCTION

6

Arsenic & Victorian Paper Hangings

CHAPTER ONE

24

Arsenic Murder & Myth

CHAPTER TWO

56

Madness in the Method; Poison in the Process

CHAPTER THREE

88

Arsenic in the Home

CHAPTER FOUR

120

The Wallpaper Designers

CHAPTER FIVE

152

The Public Debate

CHAPTER SIX

184

Getting Away from It All

CHAPTER SEVEN

216

The Rise of Arsenic-free Wallpaper

REFERENCES

248

Sources of Illustrations, Index & Acknowledgments

PLATES

8	PLATES I
	Ruby, Scarlet, Salmon
40	PLATES II
	Corn, Yellow Ochre, Khaki
72	PLATES III
	Peach, Citron, Citrine
104	PLATES IV
	Vermillion, Saffron, Apricot
136	PLATES V
	Olive, Sage, Moss
168	PLATES VI
	Beryl, Emerald, Aquamarine
200	PLATES VII
	Cerulean, Azure, Teal
232	PLATES VIII
	Pastel Shades & Soft Tones

Note from the editor: All wallpaper samples featured in these pages have been subjected to rigorous laboratory testing to ascertain the levels of arsenic, if any, contained within the pigments. The results are indicated as follows:
* Possible ** Probable *** Highly Likely

Arsenic has long been known to be poisonous. Discovered by Jabir ibn Hayyan in the eighth century CE, arsenic trioxide or 'white arsenic' is a tasteless, flour-like white powder that in the nineteenth century was marketed as rat poison. It became a popular murder weapon because it was easy to obtain, tasteless, lethal in small doses and hard to identify as symptoms of arsenic poisoning, such as vomiting and diarrhea, were also symptoms of food poisoning, cholera and dysentery. Arsenic has also long been used for medicinal purposes. In the first century CE, Greek physician and botanist Dioscorides recommended arsenic as an 'antiseptic' and 'astringent', and noted its efficacy in helping to form scabs over open wounds. In late eighteenth-century England, the physician Thomas Fowler concocted a solution of 1 per cent potassium arsenic ('liquor mineralis') for the treatment of fevers and headaches.

It is understandable then that the use of white arsenic in pigments, beginning with Scheele's green in 1775, was

not immediately perceived as a health hazard. For paint and dye manufacturers, arsenic was a cheap commodity that increased the brilliance and durability of pigments, especially when applied to wallpapers. The public loved the bright colours of the new wallpapers and even when they learnt that the dyes contained arsenic they did not consider the wallpapers dangerous as long as you did not lick them. Many dismissed as ludicrous the doctors who held that the wallpapers were poisonous, including English wallpaper designer William Morris, who stated that they 'were bitten as people were bitten by the witch fever'. As the nineteenth century progressed, however, awareness increased regarding the dangers of handling arsenic in factories and of breathing in arsenical dust or the arsenical gas produced by wallpapers in damp conditions. Adverse publicity and the decreasing availability of arsenic-infused pigments finally led to the development of arsenic-free papers.

This book traces the story of arsenic as murder weapon, domestic poison, health tonic, therapy and pigment enhancer and presents 275 samples of vibrant wallpaper designs produced during the nineteenth century that today have all been tested in the laboratories of the UK National Archives for arsenic content and proven positive.

Arsenic Murder & Myth

lthough its therapeutic benefits have been familiar for centuries, arsenic has a long and dark history as a murderer's poison of choice. Having no colour or taste, arsenical compounds such as arsenic trioxide (white arsenic) are highly effective and difficult to trace. There is an enduring story, probably apocryphal, that in 55 CE Nero poisoned Britannicus with arsenic in order to become emperor of Rome. More certainly, Sweden's King Erik XIV died by arsenic poisoning in 1577, at the hands of his brother. The infamous reputation of the Italian Borgia family – in particular, Lucrezia – as persistent poisoners of the Renaissance has likely been exaggerated, but in the seventeenth century an Italian woman, Giulia Toffana, enabled the murder of as many as 600 people using the cosmetic preparation named 'Acqua Toffana', which she had laced with arsenic. By the nineteenth century, there is no doubt that the general public in Europe and elsewhere was familiar with arsenic's more insidious properties.

One of the most famous suspected deaths by arsenic was that of Napoleon Bonaparte, who died on 5 May 1821 at the age of fifty-one, while exiled on the remote island of St Helena in the South Atlantic Ocean. His remarkable military career came to an ignominious end in a room

decorated with wallpaper in imperial gold and green.
Many people in France were convinced that the British
had murdered Napoleon, and when it was revealed that he
had written, only a few weeks before his death, 'I die before
my time, murdered by the British oligarchy and its hired
assassin', the rumours grew. No satisfactory explanation
for the assumed assassination was forthcoming.

In 1840, Napoleon's body was exhumed for reburial in
Paris. Although at that time arsenic was commonly used as
a preservative by embalmers and funeral parlours, observers
were reportedly shocked by just how well preserved the
body was, and arsenic poisoning was cited as the cause
of death. The idea that the British had killed him was
resurrected. Perhaps his guards, desperate to return
home from their own exile on St Helena, poisoned his
food to expedite his death? Or maybe he was poisoned
by overdosing on arsenic in the medicines he was known
to have been taking for a stomach complaint? Many
now consider it possible that he died of stomach cancer.
From the 1850s, the dangers of wallpaper impregnated with
arsenical pigments became an important issue in British
newspapers, and much was made of the fact that Napoleon
had slept in a wallpapered room, leading many to contend
that the British deliberately poisoned the former emperor
by this route. In the 1980s, tests were carried out on a
sample of wallpaper said to have been removed in the
1820s from the room in which Napoleon died. The paper
did contain arsenical pigments, but it is unlikely that this
alone brought about Napoleon's death. Indeed, some

contemporary reports ſtated that Napoleon, fearful of being poisoned, took to consuming small amounts of arsenic in later life, hoping to build his immunity to the chemical. Moreover, in 2008, teſts on locks of his hair dating from well before his incarceration also revealed the presence of arsenic – as did hair taken from his firſt wife, Joséphine de Beauharnais, and his son (by his second wife) Napoleon François Charles Joseph Bonaparte.

The rapid increase in poisonings during the 1830s and 1840s was, in part, connećted to the growth of the life insurance induſtry. Arsenic, easy to purchase and use but difficult to trace, made it a popular choice for those seeking to profit from the demise of a relative or spouse. This led to its contemporary nickname: 'inheritance powder'. Previously, moſt murders had been attributed to men, but with the realization that arsenic could empower even a frail, elderly woman to become a killer, the press began to sensationalize the trials of wives accused of poisoning their husbands with arsenic, and these women gained something of a cult following.

Suicide by arsenic poisoning was romanticized by Henry Wallis in his painting *Chatterton* (1856). Wallis depićts the British poet Thomas Chatterton with a serene expression on his face, his mouth curved in a gentle smile of release, and his ashen skin illuminated by sunlight. His corpse is draped artiſtically and sedućtively over a bed ſtrewn with rumpled clean sheets. Alongside torn drafts of his poems, lies an empty phial that had once contained arsenic; it has rolled away from his outſtretched hand into the foreground.

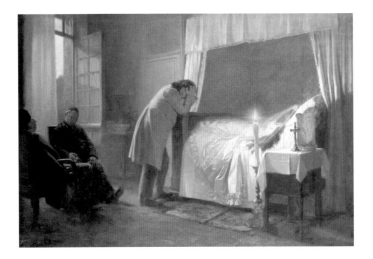

In fact, death by arsenic poisoning is a violently unpleasant
affair. In Gustave Flaubert's novel *Madame Bovary*, which
was published in the same year as Wallis's painting, Emma
is convinced the poison will let her simply fall asleep and
'all will be over'. Flaubert does not, however, romanticize
her suicide, graphically describing her death as far uglier
and more agonizing than his heroine had supposed.

A German woman, Gesche Margarethe Gottfried,
earned the sobriquet the 'Angel of Bremen' for her patient
nursing of a succession of her family and friends who
perished between 1813 and 1827. These included both her
parents, her three children, her first and second husbands,
a fiancé and her twin brother: fifteen people in all, who,
as it turned out, were all poisoned by Gottfried, perhaps in
an early case of Munchausen syndrome by proxy, in which
carers induce illness in others to gain praise and attention.
Suspicions were aroused after a doctor was asked to test some
white powder that had been found in food that Gottfried
had prepared for friends: it was arsenic. She was arrested
on 6 March 1828, and beheaded three years later, thereby
becoming the last person to be publicly executed in Bremen.

The motives of Frenchwoman Hélène Jégado are
difficult to determine. It was probably plain malice that led
her to poison upwards of thirty people in Brittany between
1833 and 1841. Between 28 June and 3 October 1833, when she
was employed as a servant to a priest in the village of Guern,

seven members of the household perished. Within the next three years, she moved to the towns of Bubry, then Locminé, poisoning ten more victims along the way. Suspicious doctors requested an autopsy of her final victim, a maid to a professor at the University of Rennes. Jégado hardly helped her case by protesting her innocence before she had actually been accused of anything. She was arrested on 1 July 1851 and executed by guillotine in Rennes on 26 February 1852.

Frequently, there was confusion over whether an arsenic poisoning was malicious or accidental because a number of foods naturally contained arsenic, and this content increased dramatically for foodstuffs grown around certain types of mines. In Britain in 1832, chemist James Marsh (1794–1846) was called to testify in court at the trial of John Bodle, accused of having poisoned his grandfather by adding arsenic to his coffee. Marsh was required to test the dead man's stomach contents. The most up-to-date examinations at the time involved either Hahnemann's test, which had been in use since the eighteenth century, or Scheele's test, devised by the same Swedish chemist, Carl Wilhelm Scheele (1742–1786), who in 1775 had invented a vivid green pigment from the compound copper arsenite, which became known as Scheele's green and was used widely in textiles and other interior decoration. When Marsh carried out Scheele's test in his laboratory, it revealed the presence of arsenic, but by the time he had transported the data to court, the results had deteriorated and the jury was unconvinced. Many years later, Bodle confessed to the murder from which he had been acquitted for lack of stable forensic evidence.

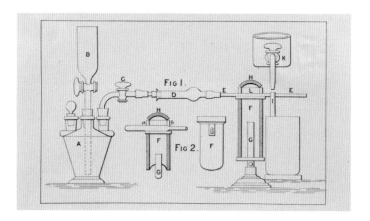

OPPOSITE *Engraved diagram showing the apparatus used in British chemist James Marsh's revolutionary forensic test for detecting the presence of arsenic.*

ABOVE RIGHT *'The 'Angel of Bremen' poisoned fifteen victims.* ABOVE LEFT *The Marsh test proved that Marie-Fortunée Lafarge killed her husband with arsenic.*

Marsh was certain that a guilty man had escaped juſtice and that Scheele's and Hahnemann's work needed to be improved. He sought to create a new teſt for arsenic, one that would ſtand up in court. In 1836, he published his successful results, and the Marsh teſt became the ſtandard procedure of checking for arsenic. He began by using Scheele's original method to produce arsine gas, but then went on to heat the gas. If arsenic was present, the heated gas left a diſtinctive residue when it made contact with a cold surface. Unlike the residue produced by the earlier teſt, the silver-black residue of the Marsh teſt (sometimes referred to as a 'mirror') did not degrade. It could therefore be preserved and used as evidence. The teſt was so sensitive that it could detect even minute amounts of arsenic. Since antimony produced a residue similar to that of arsenic, Marsh took his method one ſtage further. He proved that if the resulting residue could be dissolved by sodium hypochlorite, it was antimony; if the residue did not dissolve, it was arsenic. His teſt changed legal hiſtory.

In 1840, the sensitive and specific Marsh teſt was famously used in a French court case: the trial of a young woman, Marie-Fortunée Lafarge, accused of poisoning her elderly husband. French toxicologiſt Mathieu Orfila, a pioneer of forensic medicine who had already produced his own body of work about arsenic and was famous for his publication *A General Syſtem of Toxicology, or A Treatise on Poisons* (1814), was called as expert witness. Orfila's mere presence in court made the case a cause célèbre.

Before Marsh developed his test, Orfila had been sceptical about the number of cases in which an exhumed body had been discovered to contain arsenic. As he was quick to point out, arsenic is naturally present in soil, and the levels vary widely, so bodies could absorb arsenic after death. Whenever Orfila was required to work on a body exhumed for a post-mortem, he insisted that the soil around the grave also be tested for arsenic. In the Lafarge case, the Marsh test determined the presence of arsenic in the corpse and also confirmed that it could not have come from the soil in which it had been buried. Madame Lafarge was convicted and the Marsh test gradually was adopted worldwide.

As the nineteenth century progressed, increasing numbers of doctors began to dabble in forensic science and many were called upon as expert witnesses in court cases, especially murder trials. In 1857, Madeleine Smith, a wealthy young woman from Glasgow, was charged with poisoning her Jersey-born lover with arsenic. Pierre Emile L'Angelier was a decade older than Smith and worked as a poorly paid clerk. L'Angelier's diaries recorded their intention to marry, until he found that Smith had become engaged to a wealthy socialite named William Minnoch. Smith asked L'Angelier to return her letters; he refused and allegedly threatened to blackmail her. In his diary, L'Angelier recorded meetings with Smith at which she had served him coffee, and after which he felt ill. After L'Angelier was found dead in his lodging house on 23 March 1857, police discovered Smith's love letters and the incriminating diary and she was arrested.

After a nine-day trial, the case was declared 'not proven', and Smith was released. She left Scotland for England and married George Wardle – the business manager for the decorative arts manufacturer Morris & Company, and a good friend of well-known British artist, writer and socialist William Morris (1834–1896). In 1878, Dante Rossetti (1828–1882) wrote a darkly comic manuscript about Madeleine and Morris, whose nickname among friends was 'Topsy'. *The Death of Topsy* portrayed the Wardle children running errands for their mother, one to buy coffee and the other on a mysterious mission to a chemist's shop. The plot involved Madeleine poisoning Morris's coffee with arsenic so her husband could take over the business.

Until the mid-nineteenth century, it was possible to buy arsenic without restriction from a variety of shops and businesses; it could even be ordered by post. The most

The trial of Scottish socialite Madeleine Smith, accused of poisoning her lover, Pierre Emile L'Angelier, with arsenic in 1857, was covered by The Times, *which illustrated each stage of her story, beginning with the 'Meeting of the lovers in the laundry'.*

MEETING OF THE LOVERS IN THE LAUNDRY.

'View of the house and Madeleine Smith handing a cup of chocolate from her bedroom window to L'Angelier'. Smith was said to have offered her lover hot drinks laced with arsenic.

VIEW OF THE HOUSE AND MADELEINE SMITH HANDING A CUP OF CHOCOLATE FROM HER BED-ROOM WINDOW TO L'ANGELIER

'Visit of Miss Perry to the corpse of L'Angelier'. In his diary, L'Angelier reported telling Smith's neighbour, Mary Perry, 'I can't think why I was so unwell after getting that coffee from her... If she were to poison me, I would forgive her.'

VISIT OF MISS PERRY TO THE CORPSE OF L'ANGELIER.

'Madeleine Smith at the bar of the Justiciary, Edinburgh'. The verdict was 'not proven', rather than 'not guilty'.

MADELEINE SMITH AT THE BAR OF THE JUSTICIARY, EDINBURGH.

common reason given for buying arsenic was to kill vermin.
In 1844, French writer Alexandre Dumas commented on the
poison's astonishing availability in *The Count of Monte Cristo*:

> *Amongst us a simpleton, possessed by the demon of hate
> or cupidity, who has an enemy to destroy, or some near
> relation to dispose of, goes straight to the grocer's or
> druggist's, gives a false name, which leads more easily to
> his detection than his real one, and under the pretext that
> the rats prevent him from sleeping, purchases five or six
> grammes of arsenic – if he is really a cunning fellow, he
> goes to five or six different druggists or grocers, and thereby
> becomes only five or six times more easily traced; then,
> when he has acquired his specific, he administers duly to
> his enemy, or near kinsman, a dose of arsenic which would
> make a mammoth or mastodon burst, and which, without
> rhyme or reason, makes his victim utter groans which
> alarm the entire neighbourhood. Then arrive a crowd
> of policemen and constables. They fetch a doctor, who opens
> the dead body, and collects from the entrails and stomach
> a quantity of arsenic in a spoon. Next day a hundred
> newspapers relate the fact, with the names of the victim
> and the murderer. The same evening the grocer or grocers,
> druggist or druggists, come and say, 'It was I who sold the
> arsenic to the gentleman,' and rather than not recognize the
> guilty purchaser, they will recognize twenty. Then the foolish
> criminal is taken, imprisoned, interrogated, confronted,
> confounded, condemned, and cut off by hemp or steel; or if
> she be a woman of any consideration, they lock her up for life.*

In 1851, in Britain, the Sale of Arsenic Regulation Act was
brought into effect, preventing arsenic from being sold over
the counter (although this did not apply to its use in medicine,
agriculture or industry). One of the changes under the act
was the introduction of a poisons register, which had to be
signed whenever anyone bought arsenic. This required the
purchaser's name, address and occupation, and the date and
reason for purchase. For the first time, the act also forbade
the sale of arsenic to children. Would-be poisoners now
had to be more resourceful in the way they obtained arsenic.
France, Sweden and Prussia had already limited the
importation of products coloured with arsenic. Bavaria's
government issued an edict banning the manufacture
or sale of arsenical wallpapers in 1845. By as late as 1880,

ABOVE *'The Age of Drugs' (1900) a cartoon by Louis Dalrymple published in the satirical American magazine* Puck, *shows a pharmacist dispensing drugs, including arsenic, to an eager crowd. An advertisement on the wall announces 'The Kill 'em Quick Pharmacy', while the saloon-keeper complains 'I can't begin to compete with this fellow'.*

however, the arsenic trade remained unregulated in the United States, the Netherlands, Greece, Italy and Belgium.

In 1881, a shipboard romance led to the marriage of nineteen-year-old American Florence Chandler to a wealthy British cotton merchant, James Maybrick, who was more than twice her age. They settled in a suburb of Liverpool. Both had affairs, but Maybrick was also violent to his wife and fathered at least five children by a series of mistresses. When he was taken ill in 1889, and died soon after, his siblings became suspicious and requested a post-mortem.

Maybrick was known to take arsenic regularly, in its reputed capacity as an aphrodisiac, but the levels of arsenic in his body were much higher than expected. A servant claimed that she had seen Florence soaking flypapers in water. Hung to attract and trap flies, flypapers, a common sight in Victorian households, were impregnated with a sugary solution containing arsenic. Soaking the papers dissolved the arsenic, a method of extraction that became a common feature of crime fiction of the late nineteenth and early twentieth centuries. Florence reported that her kitchen was plagued by flies, but the servant contradicted this. On the strength of the latter's evidence, and the discovery of Florence's extramarital affairs, Florence was arrested for the murder of her husband. She swore that she had soaked the flypapers to get the arsenic for cosmetic purposes. She maintained that she was in the habit of using an arsenical face cream (see Chapter Three), and said that when she had been unable to buy it, she had decided to make her own. Florence was found guilty and sentenced to death, but her sentence was commuted and she served only fourteen years. Many were convinced of her innocence.

After her release from prison in 1904, Florence returned to the United States, where she wrote a book in which she protested her innocence and undertook a lecture tour. She had not seen her children since being imprisoned and died a lonely recluse in Connecticut in 1941. In the early 1990s, the Maybrick case again came into prominence, but this time it was attached to a new scandal. The discovery of alleged Victorian-era manuscripts led to a publishing sensation in the form of a diary, purportedly written by James, in which he claimed that he was Jack the Ripper.

Towards the end of the nineteenth century, a Dutch woman, Maria Swanenburg, nicknamed 'Goeie Mie', was uncovered as a female serial killer who favoured arsenic. Between 1860 and 1890, she took out life insurance policies in her favour in the names of dozens of her relatives and friends, and then poisoned them. She is believed to have attempted to kill 102 people by serving them arsenic in milk. Twenty-seven of her victims died and almost fifty more developed serious long-term illnesses.

LEFT *'The Tragic and Sad Story of the Maybrick Poisoning Case', in which American society wife Florence Maybrick was accused of poisoning her husband James with arsenic obtained by soaking flypapers, was covered by the* Illustrated Police News *in 1889. Dramatic vignettes depict the couple's 'First quarrel', 'Confessions of infidelity' and 'The remorse that comes too late'. In the centre is 'The affecting meeting of Mrs Maybrick and her mother in the condemned cell'.*

One of the most famous literary allusions to arsenical wallpaper can be found in the novella *The Yellow Wallpaper* (1892). In it American author Charlotte Perkins Gilman tells the story of a woman slowly driven mad by the paper in her bedroom, though it is never clear whether the wallpaper or a ghostly presence is poisoning the heroine's mind and ruining her health. The tale begins with a wife ruminating over why the grand home that she and her husband, a doctor, have rented for the summer has been made affordable to ordinary people such as themselves. The wife, who is ill, longs to be out in nature, in the '*delicious* garden', but her husband insists she needs bed rest and confines her to a bedroom in which the windows are barred. Her bedroom had once been the nursery and it is papered, badly, with vivid yellow wallpaper, as she describes:

> *It is stripped off – the paper – in great patches all round the head of my bed, about as far as I can reach … I never saw a worse paper in my life. One of those sprawling flamboyant patterns committing every artistic sin … The colour is repellent, almost revolting; a smouldering unclean yellow … This paper looks to me as if it knew what a vicious influence it had.*

The narrator's health deteriorates and she begs her husband to allow her to sleep in another room, or to remove the wallpaper, but he just laughs and orders her to take her medicines. She does not. Her maid complains that

the wallpaper stains 'everything it touched' and is starting to affect their clothes. As autumn arrives and the air becomes damp, the narrator notices a strange smell in the room. This is consistent with contemporary analyses of arsenical wallpaper poisoning cases by toxicology experts: when the wallpaper becomes damp, malodorous arsenical gas is released (see Chapter Three). By the end of the story, the narrator is convinced a woman is stuck inside the wallpaper:

> *There are things in that paper which nobody knows but me, or ever will. Behind that outside pattern the dim shapes get clearer every day. It is always the same shape, only very numerous. And it is like a woman stooping down and creeping about behind that pattern.*

Convinced the woman is mocking her, she locks herself inside the room and throws away the key. She then bites and rips the wallpaper from the walls with her teeth, to prevent the woman from reaching her. The contemporary assumption was that this was a tale of insanity; modern readers interpret it as a portrait of a woman stifled by her era.

In 1892, the same year in which *The Yellow Wallpaper* was published, Oscar Wilde's play *Lady Windermere's Fan* opened in London. The playwright appeared at the theatre wearing an arsenic-green carnation in his buttonhole.

When asked what it signified, he replied that it meant nothing. Two years later, a novel was published anonymously, titled *The Green Carnation*. The author was Robert Smythe Hichens, a friend of Wilde and his lover, Bosie (Lord Alfred Douglas), but the press maintained that it had been written by Wilde. The two main characters in the story, Esmé Amarinth and Lord Reggie Hastings, were caricatures of Wilde and Bosie. The novel explains the arsenical origin of the buttonhole thus:

> *'And who started the fashion of the green carnation?'*
> *'That was Mr Amarinth's idea. He calls it the arsenic*
> *flower of an exquisite life. He wore it, in the first instance,*
> *because it blended so well with the colour of absinthe.'*

In 1895, a year after the novel was published, Wilde was arrested. Hichens, who had intended the novel as friendly parody rather than criticism of homosexuality, removed the book from circulation, terrified it would be used against his friend. It was not published again until 1948. During Wilde's later trial, the green carnation became considered sinister. Much was made of the 'unnatural' aspect of a green flower. Years later it was claimed that the green carnation had been a secret symbol used by homosexual men. In reality, it simply allowed Wilde to shock the general public.

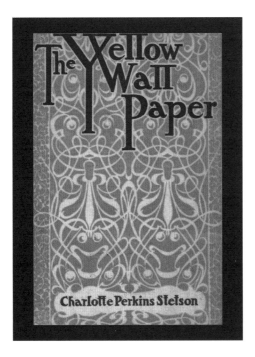

LEFT The Yellow Wallpaper *(1892) a novella by Charlotte Perkins Gilman (Stetson was her married name), describes the gradual descent into madness of a woman who is confined by her husband in a room covered in patterned yellow wallpaper. She begins to hallucinate and notices a strange smell. This corresponds to toxicology reports of wallpaper containing arsenical pigments emitting a distinctive-smelling gas in damp conditions.*

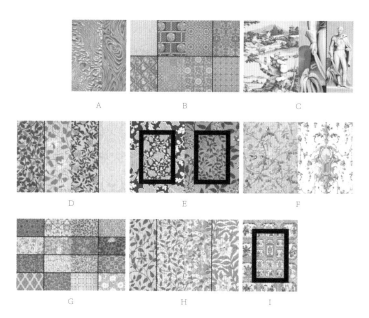

A · · · · · · · · · · · · B · · · · · · · · · · · · · · · · C

D · · · · · · · · · · · · E · · · · · · · · · · · · · · · · F

G · · · · · · · · · · · · H · · · · · · · · · · · · · · · · I

A   1. ••• *Mid brown*. Richard Goodlad & Company, Newcastle-on-Tyne, UK, 1856
B   1. ••• *Yellow*. Jules Desfossé, Paris, France, 1878 | 2. •• *Light brown*. Christopher
    Dresser for William Cooke, Leeds, 1879 | 3. ••• *Green*. William Cooke, Leeds, UK,
    1880 | 4. •• *Yellow, dark green, brown*. William Woollams & Company, London, 1880
    5. •• *Dark & light green*. Christopher Dresser for William Cooke, Leeds, 1879 6. •••
    Dark & light brown. Jules Desfossé, Paris, 1880 | 7. ••• *Brown*. Cole & Sons, London,
    1883 | 8. •• *Brown, green*. William Cooke, Leeds, UK, 1878
C   1. ••• *Dark brown*. Trumble & Cooke, Leeds, UK, 1852 | 2. ••• *Dark brown*.
    Charles Walker Norwood, London, 1852
D   1. ••• *Dark green, brown*. William Cooke, Leeds, UK, 1879 | 2. •• *Dark green*.
    Ibid., 1879 | 3. ••• *Yellow*. Ibid., 1879 | 4. ••• *Yellow*. John Mair, Son & Company,
    London, 1878
E   1. ••• *Yellow*. Richard Goodlad & Company, Newcastle-on-Tyne, UK, 1856
    2. ••• *Dark green, brown*. William Cooke, Leeds, UK, 1879
F   1. ••• *Green*. Jules Desfossé, Paris, France, 1879 | 2. ••• *Brown, yellow, purple*.
    James Toleman, London, 1847
G   1. ••• *Orange*. William Cooke, Leeds, UK, 1879 | 2. ••• *Brown, beige*.
    Christopher Dresser for William Woollams & Company, London 1863 | 3. ••• *Mid
    green*. Lightbown, Aspinall & Company, Lancashire, UK, 1881 | 4. ••• *Green*. Ibid., 1881
    5. ••• *Orange, brown*. Ibid., 1881 | 6. ••• *Dark yellow*. Robert Christie, London, 1877
    7. ••• *Dark beige*. Christopher Dresser for William Cooke, Leeds, UK, 1863
    8. ••• *Yellow, beige, brown*. William Cooke, Leeds, 1880 | 9. ••• *Yellow, brown*.
    Ibid., 1879 | 10. ••• *Green*. Ibid., 1878 | 11. •• *Yellow, red*. Ibid., 1880
    12. •• *Yellow*. Ibid., 1879 | 13. ••• *Yellows*. Ibid., 1879 | 14. •• *Dark green, brown*. Ibid., 1880
    15. •• *Mid green*. Ibid., 1878 | 16. •• *Yellow, white*. Lightbown, Aspinall & Company,
    Lancashire, 1881
H   1. ••• *Peach, green, dark green line, gold*. William Cooke, Leeds, UK, 1879
    2. •• *Dark green*. Ibid., 1879 | 3. ••• *Green with pale cream line*. Ibid., 1880 | 4. •• *Yellow,
    cream, brown*. Ibid., 1880
I   1. ••• *Yellow*. C. E. & J. G. Potter, Lancashire, UK, 1873

TOXICITY OF PAPERS: • POSSIBLE   •• PROBABLE   ••• HIGHLY LIKELY

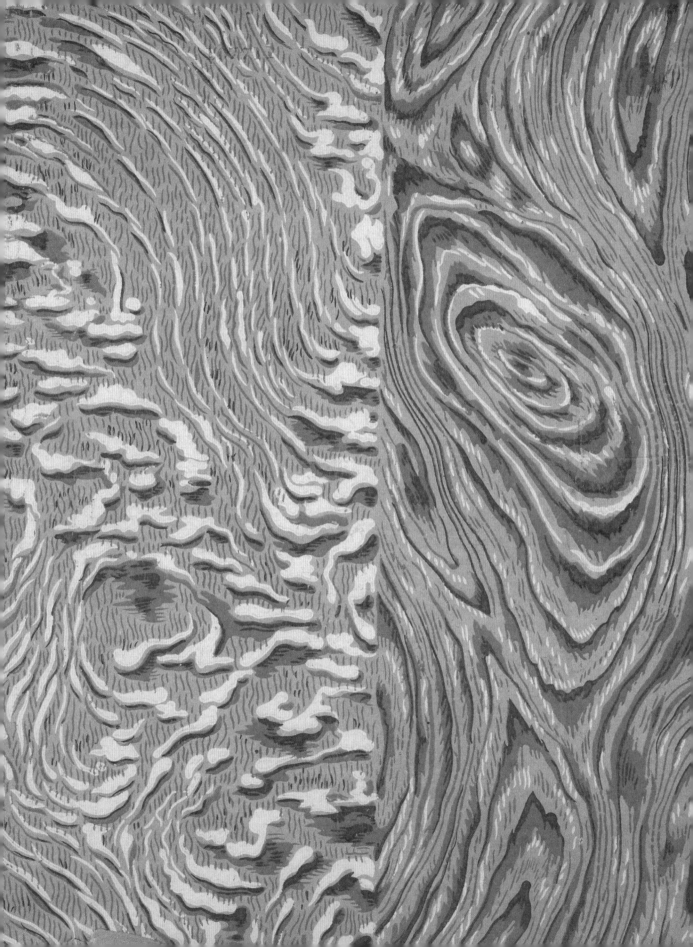

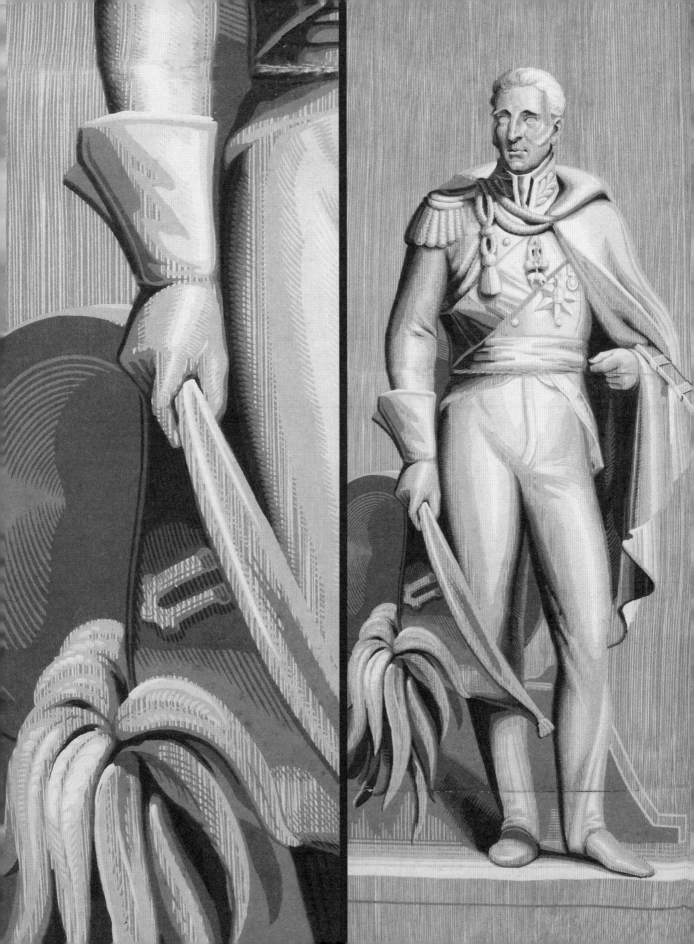

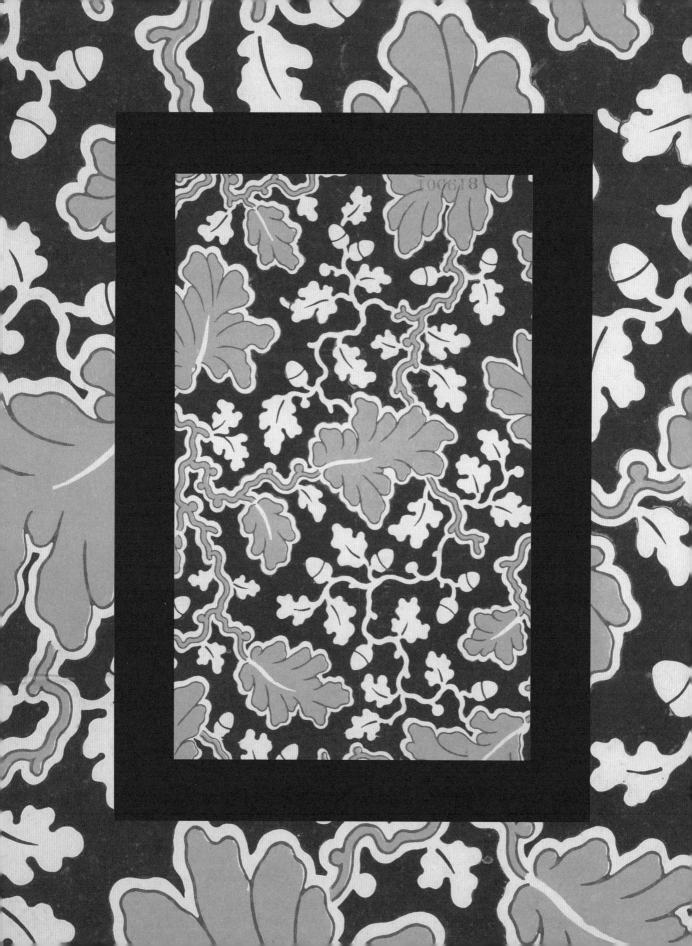

OPPOSITE *Encylopaedia illustration of a British mine in the 1860s. The new blasting and drilling methods exposed miners to arsenic dust and toxic waste materials.*

ABOVE LEFT *Nineteenth-century illustration of ores, including arsenical red realgar and yellow orpiment.* ABOVE *Yellow sulphide of arsenic (orpiment).*

one mine owner might come as a surprise. William Morris is remembered today as being fervently against mass production: he spearheaded the Arts and Crafts Movement in an effort to save skills that the Industrial Revolution was fast rendering obsolete. In addition, he set up his own company in which all the workers received fair wages and enjoyed excellent working conditions. One of his most oft-repeated quotations is 'I do not want art for a few, any more than education for a few, or freedom for a few.' Yet the personal wealth of his family was derived from one of the world's largest producers of arsenic: Devon Great Consols. Morris's father, who died when William was a child, left him shares in the mine (near Tavistock, in Devon). It was his father's lucky speculation in the mines during the 1840s that funded Morris's education as well as his early business ventures, including the creation of Morris, Marshall, Faulkner & Company in 1861. In 1871, Morris became one of the directors of Devon Great Consols, a position he retained for four years. Around 1872, during his time as a director, he wrote to his mother that Devon Great Consols had a 'new contract for arsenic, & got a very good price for it'.

One of the great unanswered questions about Morris is why he never visited the mines or concerned himself with the welfare of the miners and their families. It seems

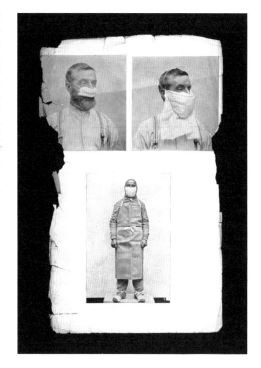

extraordinarily out of character for a man known to be generous and philanthropic, and to genuinely care about the welfare of his workers (see Chapters Four and Six).

Morris must have been acquainted with the atrocious working conditions at the mines because, in the early 1860s, Devon Great Consols had been the subject of an investigation that had been reported in the newspapers. Even if, as a shareholder and newspaper reader, Morris had somehow managed to remain oblivious to the journalistic fervour surrounding Devon Great Consols, he cannot have been unaware that his own uncle, Thomas Morris, had been interviewed for the investigation committee's report. Thomas had admitted that boys were sent down mine shafts from the age of ten, and that girls as young as eight were employed to sort through the refuse heaps that included arsenic; he also admitted that health problems suffered by the adult workers were caused by their jobs. One well-known ill effect was the lesions known as arsenic 'pocks', but many workers actually died from lung disease brought about by arsenic poisoning.

A letter sent by William Morris to his wife, Jane, in 1881 while visiting his married sister Alice in South Devon proves that he did travel close enough to the mines to have inspected

them in person, although by this date he was no longer a director and had sold his shares. In the letter he reported that he and Alice had strolled together beside the River Tavy – only a few miles from the site of the Devon Great Consols mines.

In later years, Morris spoke to poet, journalist and traveller Wilfrid Scawen Blunt about his own involvement with the mines. In 1896, the year of Morris's death, Blunt recorded this earlier conversation in his diary. It seems that Morris was economical about his involvement with Devon Great Consols, telling Blunt, 'We had some mining shares in Cornwall, and when I succeeded to them, I sold them. My relations thought me both wicked and mad, but the shares are worth nothing now.' In fact, having succeeded to the shares when he came of age in 1855, Morris sold the bulk of them between 1874 and 1877; he also judiciously sold them at a time when copper mining was heading towards a slump.

Masks and overalls were of only limited use in preventing a worker from coming into contact with arsenic. The physical effects of this exposure could be horrific. Direct contact could lead to the fingernails turning a yellow colour, and greenish, ulcerated lesions (or 'pocks') might open up on the skin of the hands. Sensitive areas, such as lips and nostrils, were prone to become raw and reddish in the presence of arsenic. Any scratches or abrasions in the skin made the effects even worse. In 1863, the *Fife Herald* reported on the health of the mine workers who produced arsenic, and that of the factory workers who manufactured the arsenic-green pigments:

> *The men working in the cobalt mines of Germany are greatly affected by it (cobalt containing a large proportion of the poison); and in former times, a prayer used regularly to be offered up in the German churches that God would preserve miners from cobalt and spirits. In all the manufactures in which emerald green is employed it is dangerous to life, and produces almost certain injury to the constitution. In open air manufactories its effects are, as might be expected, least marked. But even there the workmen are invariably affected with boils and pimples; itching in, and an acrid discharge from the nostrils ...*

All the more remarkable, then, that such a substance should have been so prevalent in nineteenth-century

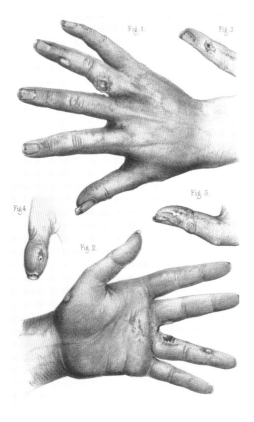

LEFT *Illustration from a French medical journal in 1859 showing typical damage caused to hands by exposure to arsenical dyes. The skin is discoloured, both as a result of the poison in the bloodstream and the staining effect of the green dye itself. Characteristic skin lesions, small keratoses and patchy areas of hyperpigmentation are evident.*

Chemische-u.Farben-Fabrik zu Schonungen.

homes. One reason that arsenic became so commonly used in interior decoration during this period was due to the development by Swedish chemist Carl Scheele in 1775 of the vivid green pigment known as Scheele's green, made from the compound copper arsenite. Its depth of colour and superb pigmentation properties made Scheele's green highly sought after by clothing and interiors manufacturers. When ground with oil to make paint, its sea-green colour made it popular in the decoration of ships' cabins.

Even before Scheele's green became common in Britain, however, questions were being raised in Germany about the side effects of arsenical pigments in domestic decoration, since the poisonous properties of arsenic were well known. In 1815, German chemist Leopold Gmelin (1788–1853) reported in a Berlin newspaper that the use of arsenical pigments in wallpaper was dangerous, and recommended a ban. Gmelin began to record a strange odour that he described as 'mouse-like'. It was released in damp conditions by wallpapers coloured with Scheele's green, and he identified it as arsenical gas. In 1839, Gmelin published an article in a popular Sunday newspaper, *Karlsruher Zeitung*, warning readers against using Scheele's green. British manufacturers ignored his concerns – as well as those that Scheele himself had voiced several years earlier. It took many years before Gmelin's work was recognized outside Germany.

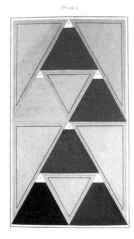
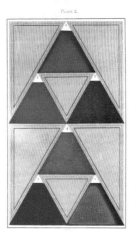

In 1814, German industrialist Wilhelm Sattler (1784–1859) set out to improve Scheele's green, which, because of its copper content, had a tendency to fade and blacken over time. He succeeded in creating a deeper, more durable and opaque shade of green from arsenic and verdigris at his dye and white lead company in Schweinfurt, Germany. Known as emerald green, Paris green or Schweinfurt green, it became hugely popular with painters, clothing manufacturers, wallpaper designers, dyers and confectioners.

As the nineteenth century wore on, many more arsenical pigments were developed, offering superior vividness and durability. In his essay 'The Walls and Wall-Coverings' (1883), British architect Robert W. Edis noted: 'It may be mentioned here that green is not the only tint in which arsenical colouring is to be feared. I believe that lilac, certain shades of blue, pink and French grey all contain arsenic to a certain extent.' Indeed, by the 1890s, yellows, golds, golden browns and whites were equally rich in the poison.

In late Georgian and early Regency Britain, domestic colour palettes tended to be understated in tone, but tastes in colour changed with the decades, accompanied by changes in interior decoration. In 1845, David Ramsay Hay produced his influential illustrated theory of colour harmony, *A Nomenclature of Colours, Hues, Tints, and Shades, Applicable to the Arts and Natural Sciences; to Manufactures, and other Purposes of General Utility*. Over the course of 240 colour plates, Hay illustrated his theory of colour coordination, which was based on aesthetic principles, rather than on relationships between neighbouring hues. During the 1850s, the taste for more vibrant wall and textile colours developed apace. A particularly striking example of a vivid green can be seen in a painting of the biblical character Mary Magdalene by Pre-Raphaelite painter Frederick Sandys in *c.* 1859. Sandys painted his red-haired model against the background of a richly patterned green wall, presaging the Aesthetic movement's fascination with green from the 1860s onwards.

In the eighteenth century, all wallpaper had been produced painstakingly on relatively small, individual sheets of paper. These were decorated by hand, usually by block-printing, in which, typically, a wooden block was fastened to a table, a design carved into it and coloured paint applied. The paper was then laid over the block and pressed into the carved contours with a roller; alternatively, the block might be lowered onto the paper and hammered down with mallets to transfer the design. Detailed colour work could then be added with a paintbrush. In the early 1800s, however, mechanization began to change how wallpaper was produced. In 1785, French-German industrialist Christophe-Philippe Oberkampf invented a machine for printing dyes on paper. Then, in 1799, Louis-Nicolas Robert, who was working in Paris, patented a machine to produce wallpaper in long, continuous rolls. Adverse economic conditions meant that it was not taken up in France,

LEFT Mary Magdalene *(c. 1859) by Frederick Sandys has a background of fashionable emerald green Victorian wallpaper, which very likely would have contained arsenic.*

OPPOSITE *Colour plates from David Ramsay Hay's* A Nomenclature of Colours (1845) *which was influential in developing the taste for vivid colour schemes, which encouraged the use of arsenical pigments.*

but patents for the development of Robert's invention were purchased in London in 1801, backed by stationers Henry and Sealy Fourdrinier. Four years later, a machine was produced that was capable of running out rolls 27 feet long by 4 feet wide.

Roller printing significantly speeded up the process of wallpaper production. Instead of re-inking the block for each new printing, the surface of the roller was raised and automatically recharged with paint from a trough. By 1819, the British wallpaper industry had begun to embrace technological changes, although not everyone was as content with these improvements as the factory owners. In 1839, interior decorator John Gregory Crace bemoaned in a speech to the Royal Institute of British Architects what he considered to be the 'degeneracy' of modern wallpaper designers. Yet the nineteenth century would become one of the most exciting periods in wallpaper production, peopled with brilliantly creative designers, architects and interior decorators. British and French companies dominated, with North American designers and manufacturers only establishing themselves towards the end of the century.

Wallpaper designs were not limited to the birds, fruits and flowers motifs that are familiar today. Also common were extensive landscapes and designs featuring bold geometric prints, as well as lozenge-shaped motifs that resemble Art Deco patterns from the 1920s but actually date back to the early 1840s, in vibrant colours. In the United States, arabesques, chinoiserie and neoclassical motifs were very popular, later giving way to geometric patterning and Gothic Revival design. Wallpaper designs could also be informative or commemorative. Children's wallpapers included images from well-known stories or nursery rhymes, often accompanied by text to help them learn to read.

London had been the centre for wallpaper production prior to the 1840s, but as the industry became increasingly mechanized, it spread to the provinces. The new technology included machines powered by foot pedals, which made it much easier and quicker to print the paper than the old methods had allowed, and steam-powered machines that could print colours straight onto long rolls of paper in one movement and then dry them. These inventions, combined with the halving of the tax on paper in 1836 (it was abolished altogether in 1861), made it possible for all but the poorest households to afford wallpaper. By the 1850s, it was possible to print complex patterns using up to eight different colours at the same time. In Britain, production rose by more than 2,615 per cent, from 1,222,753 rolls in 1834 to 32,000,000 rolls by 1874. Tens of thousands of feet of printed wallpapers could now be made in one factory in a single day, and complex colour combinations were prevalent. In 1883, one commentator in *The Journal of Decorative Art* noted approvingly: 'To see a piece of paper go in at one end of a machine plain, and come out on the other side printed in twenty colours, all complete, is a very wonderful sight.'

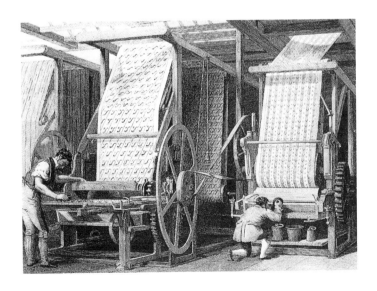

The specialized workforce that had previously made the paper hangings swiftly found their skills made redundant by these technological advances. Those who kept their jobs were only required to feed the machinery with paper and pigments and to ensure that the machines were in working order. Factory owners readily hired child labourers, whose small hands and fingers proved useful for cleaning out the intricacies of machinery. The health of these children was of little concern to most of their employers, who could pay a child worker half of that paid to an adult.

In 1833, in Britain, a Royal Commission was created to look into the conditions at factories. The shocking results helped to bring about wide-ranging changes. One witness interviewed was a labourer named Charles Aberdeen. He told the Commission, 'I have seen men and women that have worked in a factory all their lives, like myself, and that get married; and I have seen the race become diminutive and small; I have myself had seven children, not one of which survived six weeks; my wife is an emaciated person, like myself, a little woman, and she worked during her childhood, younger than myself, in a factory.' The inquiry resulted in the Factory Act of 1833, which improved the conditions of child labourers in Britain. Unfortunately, as a result, many adults had to work longer to compensate for the loss of the young workforce.

WALL-PAPER PRINTING MACHINE.   495

MACHINE FOR PRINTING IN TWENTY COLOURS.

LEFT *Paint troughs hold twenty different colours in this rotary wallpaper printing machine depicted in a trade magazine in 1877.*

OPPOSITE *A French flock wallpaper from the 1770s. Flock, a byproduct of the wool industry, was applied to wallpaper to duplicate the appearance of damask or velvet and became highly fashionable in the nineteenth century. Workers who produced these papers suffered respiratory problems from exposure to flocking dust.*

By the 1840s, although there was legislation addressing workers' injuries from mechanical accidents, there was none to protect those employed in inhospitable environments such as wallpaper factories. Workers suffered from chemical fumes given off by the synthetic colours, which caused breathing and skin problems, and many of those working in the 'steam drying' rooms found their skin, eyes and lungs affected by the heat, humidity and chemical gases produced by the printing process. In factories that used arsenic-based pigments to colour papers, the repercussions could be even more serious. Workers whose job involved crushing the pigments to release the colour risked arsenic poisoning every day. As late as 1888, a visitor to a factory in Kent, UK, where Schweinfurt green was used, complained of motes of pigment in the atmosphere: 'The air was filled with it. I could hardly breathe.'

Flock wallpaper (invented by Jerome Lanyer as early as 1634) enjoyed a newly fashionable status in the nineteenth century. The Prince Consort had his bedroom in Balmoral Castle decorated with a green flock paper with gold fleur-de-lis, produced by William Cooke. Factory owners were keen to meet the demand, which created yet more health problems for their workers. The flocking, which gives the paper its raised texture, is made from tiny pieces of wool or cotton. The air inside factories became thick with flocking dust, which caused lung problems and even asphyxiation. It got into the workers' eyes, hair, mouths, noses and the creases of their skin as well as under their fingernails.

WALL PAPER MANUFACTORY
JANEWAY & CARPENDER.

Wallpapers, or 'paper hangings', had initially been sold (and manufactured) by stationers, but by the mid-eighteenth century many upholstery firms were also offering them. At that time, as Robert Campbell noted in *The London Tradesman* (1747), an upholsterer would offer to design rooms for customers and also supply the decorative materials and workmen. Paper samples were available to view in a paper-hanging warehouse and were supplied to the customer in due course. Alternatively, a supplier might propose certain papers: in 1819, London decorators Duppa, Slodden & Company advised one customer: 'We have selected a few patterns for your inspection ... and beg to say that any of them can be made in a week or ten days.' They added that they would be more than willing to supply a labourer to apply it, too – even though the customer in question lived in Wales.

With increasing urbanization and a relative increase in affluence, demand for wallpaper rose. In 1883, the firm Heywood, Higginbottom & Smith announced that it was now manufacturing 6 million rolls each year. By the turn of the century, larger firms such as William Woollams & Company and Lightbown, Aspinall & Company might need to keep a stock of 8,000 large rolls on hand. In order to meet the increasing call for wallpaper, modest independent shops appeared, although even towards the end of the nineteenth century retailers were not plentiful. Successful manufacturers such as Jeffrey & Company and Essex & Company had

their own showrooms, which displayed the full range
of their products. However, they were aimed at trade
customers, not the general public, and were located in
London, the original heart of the British wallpaper industry.
Still, these emporia were evidence of the increasing artistic
worth with which wallpapers were now regarded. One
visitor to Sanderson's London showroom in 1895 marvelled:

> [The] walls were covered with papers of a magnificence,
> of a beauty, such as we had never imagined ... papers
> suitable for the walls of drawing room, for bed-chamber,
> or of sober library ... papers displayed in handsome pattern
> books where every page you turned gave up a specimen
> more graceful in conception, more original in style
> and treatment, than the one you looked at last.

Wealthy customers might buy papers from their
own decorators, who often kept bound pattern books,
first available in the late nineteenth century, showing
a manufacturer's entire latest collection. In addition
to wallpapers, customers could buy a full range of
household furniture from firms such as Liberty and
Maples, which effectively acted as interior designers,
recalling the complete service offered by eighteenth-
century upholstery companies.

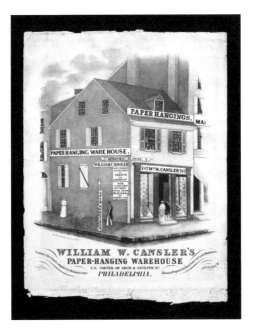

LEFT *Wallpapers
(or 'paper hangings')
were originally sold
by stationers and
upholsterers until
specialist independent
shops such as this
American firm,
advertised c. 1845,
began to appear in the
nineteenth century as
consumer appetite for
wallpaper increased.*

OPPOSITE *Large-
scale mechanized
factories, such as that
of American wallpaper
manufacturer Janeway
& Carpender, c. 1880,
met the increased
demand.*

A   B   C

D   E   F

G   H   I

A   1. ** *Yellow*. William Cooke, Leeds, UK, 1880
B   1. ** *Dark green*. William Cooke, Leeds, UK, 1881 | 2. *** *Yellow, red, brown*. Ibid., 1881
     3. *** *Brown, green*. Ibid., 1881 | 4. *** *Yellow, brown*. Ibid., 1881 | 5. *** *Yellow*. Ibid., 1880
     6. *** *Dark green*. Lightbown, Aspinall & Company, Lancashire, UK, 1881
     7. *** *Brown, gold, light yellow/brown*. William Cooke, Leeds, UK, 1881
     8. *** *Yellow*. Ibid., 1881
C   1. *** *Dark brown, yellow, beige*. Wilcoxon & Sons, London, 1847 | 2. *** *Yellow,
     yellow/brown*. William Cooke, Leeds, UK, 1881 | 3. *** *Brown, beige*. Corbière,
     Son & Brindle, London, 1877 | 4. *** *Brown*. Jules Desfossé, Paris, France, 1878
D   1. *** *Dark green*. William Cooke, Leeds, UK, 1879 | 2. ** *Green*. Ibid., 1880 | 3. ***
     Green. Ibid., 1880 | 4. ** *Dark green*. Ibid., 1881
E   1. ** *Yellow, blue*. Jeffrey & Company, London, 1878 | 2. *** *Yellow, brown*.
     Jules Desfossé, Paris, France, 1880
F   1. *** *Pale green, cream*. William Cooke, Leeds, UK, 1879 | 2. *** *Cream*. Ibid., 1880
G   1. ** *Beige*. William Cooke, Leeds, UK, 1879 | 2. *** *Brown*. Ibid., 1881 | 3. *** *Green,
     brown*. Ibid., 1880 | 4. ** *Brown, cream*. Ibid., 1881 | 5. *** *Green, brown lines*. Ibid., 1881
     6. *** *Dark green border*. Ibid., 1881
H   1. *** *Brown, yellow/brown, black, metallic gold*. William Cooke, Leeds, UK, 1881
     2. ** *Dark green, black, metallic gold*. Ibid., 1881 | 3. *** *Yellow/brown, black, orange,
     yellow*. Ibid., 1881 | 4. *** *Dark green leaf*. Ibid., 1880 | 5. *** *Yellow/brown*. Ibid., 1881
     6. *** *Brown, pale yellow, metallic gold*. Ibid., 1879 | 7. *** *Cream*. Ibid., 1880 | 8. ***
     Yellows. Ibid., 1880 | 9. *** *Yellow/brown/peach*. Ibid., 1881 | 10. *** *Green/brown*. Ibid.,
     1881 | 11. *** *Dark green*. Ibid., 1881 | 12. ** *Brown*. Ibid., 1880 | 13. *** *Yellow/brown*. Ibid.,
     1879 | 14. ** *Yellow*. Ibid., 1879 | 15. ** *Dark green*. Ibid., 1881 | 16. *** *Cream*. Ibid., 1879
     17. ** *Red, blue*. Corbière & Sons, London, 1878 | 18. * *Yellow, gold, red*. William Cooke,
     Leeds, UK, 1880 | 19. ** *Dark green*. Ibid., 1880 | 20. *** *Brown/green*. Ibid., 1880
I   1. *** *Yellow, blue, green, pink*. Alexander J. Duff, London, UK, 1880

TOXICITY OF PAPERS: * POSSIBLE   ** PROBABLE   *** HIGHLY LIKELY

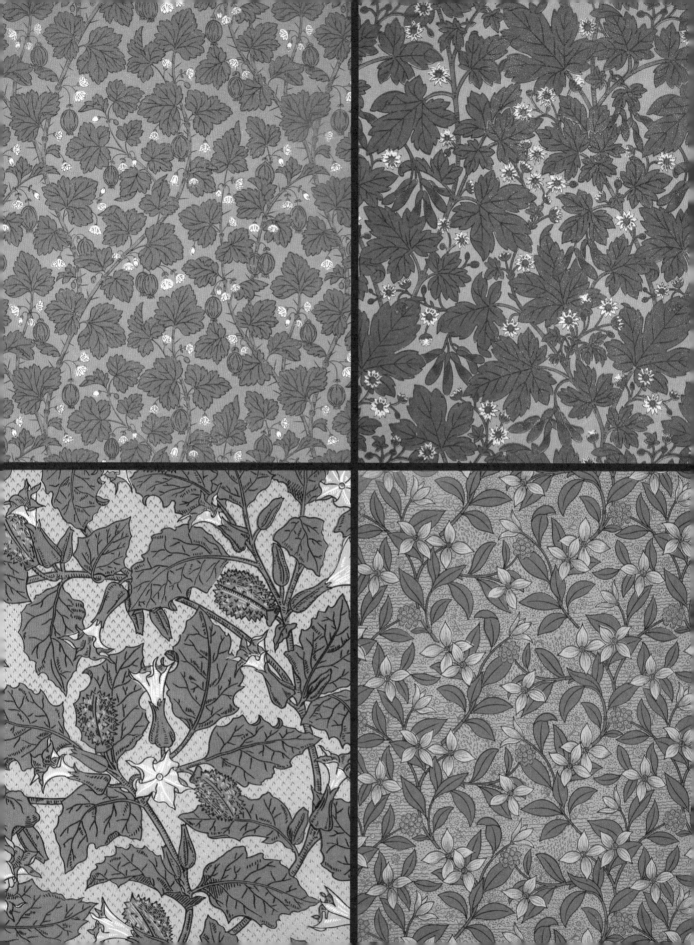

CHAPTER THREE

Arsenic in the Home

y the middle of the nineteenth century, arsenic could be found in a variety of guises throughout the home. Nearly every household had a good supply of arsenic powder on hand for use as a mouse and rat poison. People ate fruit and vegetables sprayed with arsenic-based insecticides, such as Paris green (so named after the use of the chemical to kill rats in the sewers and slums of Paris), and meat from animals that were regularly dipped in arsenic as a fly deterrent. Arsenic was also present in cleaning products, in the dyes used in curtains, lampshades and wallpaper, in health tonics and also in cosmetics, candles and clothing. Women and girls wore gloves, hats, and stockings and carried silk handkerchiefs dyed with arsenical pigments. Children opened presents wrapped in paper containing arsenic and played with toys decorated with paint containing arsenic. Arsenic, lead, plaster of Paris and other poisons and contaminants were all used quite openly in the preparation or colouring of certain foods. Newspapers regularly printed cautionary tales of arsenic powder having been mistaken by an illiterate kitchen maid for flour, baking powder or icing sugar. Despite the toxic element's domestic ubiquity, panic broke out in Britain in 1879, when it was discovered that lickable postage stamps were coloured with arsenical dyes.

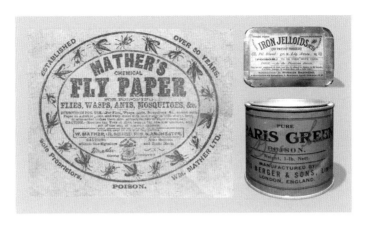

OPPOSITE *Fowler's solution, a health tonic (left) and cosmetic 'complexion wafers' (right) both contained arsenic, which was said to have beneficial effects.*

ABOVE *Victorian arsenical household products included flypapers (left), iron tablets (top right) and Paris green, a rodent and insect poison (below right).*

Strangely, few people seemed able to make the connection between rat poison containing arsenic and the arsenic used for other day-to-day purposes.

Arsenic first became a common household product with the eighteenth-century health remedy known as Fowler's solution. The invention of a British doctor from Staffordshire, Thomas Fowler, Fowler's solution contained around 1 per cent arsenic trioxide. In 1786, he published his findings into the curative effects of arsenic in *Medical Reports of the Effects of Arsenic in the Cure of Agues, Remitting Fevers and Periodic Headaches*. It caused an instant sensation and made him famous. Soon Fowler's solution was being heralded as a miraculous cure-all for everything from asthma and eczema to dysentery and lymphoma. It was also discovered to be especially beneficial in the treatment of syphilis, a highly prevalent sexually transmitted disease for which previously there had not been an effective cure. Ironically, the arsenic cure that had once been offered for syphilis was also taken by millions of Victorian men as an aphrodisiac. The unwanted side effects of taking Fowler's solution were not recognized as signs of arsenic poisoning for many decades, and Fowler's recipe continued to be sold and experimented with well into the twentieth century.

In addition to Fowler's solution, many of the era's most popular beauty products contained arsenic, including face cream and 'medicated arsenic complexion soap', which imparted a desirable luminosity to the skin by destroying

red blood cells. Women also happily ate 'safe arsenic complexion wafers'. One advertisement for the wafers described them as being for those who 'desire a transparent, clear, fresh complexion, free from blotch, blemish, roughness, coarseness, redness, freckles or pimples'. H. B. Fould of New York manufactured a thirty-day treatment of Dr Campbell's safe arsenic complexion wafers to be taken daily along with the use of Fould's medicated arsenic soap, for the same period – and all for one dollar. The Union Manufacturing & Agency Company of Melbourne, meanwhile, promised 'Complexions like alabaster and roses' to those who purchased their arsene pilules (arsenical pills).

Throughout the nineteenth century, newspaper articles appeared concerning the 'peasant arsenic-eaters' of Styria (now in Austria). One sixty-year-old man was reported to have incrementally increased his intake to four grains per day, usually considered a fatal dose. Much was made of the discovery of the Styrians, who took arsenic daily in the belief that it improved their health or appearance. Every few years, a journalist would resurrect the story, thereby keeping it alive in the public consciousness. Reports abounded of the peasants' bright eyes, unblemished complexions and ability to climb mountains without suffering from altitude sickness or breathlessness. As each new spate of articles promoted the benefits of arsenic, doctors would warn that only the smallest dose should be taken, and many cited tales of patients who had increased their mild dose with fatal consequences. Professor J. Alfred Wanklyn wrote about the Styrians in his book *Arsenic* (1901):

> *Arsenic-eaters, as might be expected, commence the practice of arsenic-eating by taking small doses of common arsenic. Less than half-grain doses are taken to begin with, two or three times in the week. The dose is very gradually and cautiously increased until it reaches about two grains; and this practise of arsenic-eating may be continued for forty years without apparent detriment to the system.*

Long before the scandal of poisonous wallpaper pigments became a matter of public discussion, angry articles appeared in the British press about the ready

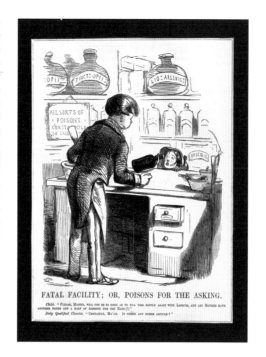

FATAL FACILITY; OR, POISONS FOR THE ASKING.

Child. "PLEASE, MISTER, WILL YOU BE SO GOOD AS TO FILL THIS BOTTLE AGAIN WITH LODNUM, AND LET MOTHER HAVE ANOTHER POUND AND A HALF OF ARSENIC FOR THE RATS(!)"

Duly Qualified Chemist. "CERTAINLY, MA'AM. IS THERE ANY OTHER ARTICLE?"

availability of the poison. Between the 1840s and the 1860s, caricaturist John Leech produced a number of poignant cartoons in the popular magazine *Punch*. In a world in which a large percentage of the population was illiterate, cartoons were an effective way of conveying information to thousands of customers. Leech's images were not only meant to amuse, but also to inform the public about the dangers of the poison. In 1849, he drew a cartoon entitled 'Fatal Facility; or, Poisons for the Asking'. It depicts a child at a shop counter being served by a 'duly qualified chemist'. The child is asking for laudanum for her mother and 'another pound and a half of arsenic for the rats(!)'. Behind the shopkeeper, shelves are filled with jars of opium and liquid arsenic. A sign promises 'All sorts of poisons constantly on sale'.

Nine years later, Leech drew 'The Great Lozenge-Maker. A Hint to Paterfamilias' (1858), about a recent scandal in Bradford, England, in which a number of people, including many children, had been fatally poisoned by sweets made with arsenic. On 9 November 1858, the *Leeds Mercury* reported that Charles Hodgson of Shipley, his assistant William Goddard and confectioner Joseph Neal had been tried for the manslaughter of seven-year-old Elizabeth Mary Midgley. She had died after eating

peppermint drops, but the sweets were actually 'composed of arsenious acid, sugar, starch and gum', according to analysis by chemist Felix Marsh Rimmington. In court, Rimmington revealed that a single lozenge had contained '11 ¼ grains of arsenious acid'. Elizabeth was only one of around 200 victims who became ill after eating the sweets; seventeen of whom died. Eleven of the dead were children; the youngest was seventeen months old.

The adulteration of basic foods with cheap bulking and colouring agents, many of which would never have been approved for consumption, was a regular concern of social campaigners. Leech's 'The Great Lozenge-Maker' cartoon is not concerned only with arsenic, but also with all the harmful additives used by unscrupulous manufacturers. It is set in the interior of a sweet shop, in which a clothed adult skeleton is stirring a cauldron-like saucepan. Nearby shelves hold containers labelled 'bon bons for juvenile parties' and 'all sorts'. On the floor stand a huge barrel of arsenic and a large tub of plaster of Paris; instead of spoons, the barrel needs a trowel and the tub a spade for measuring the ingredients into the pan.

In 1851, Charles Dickens's magazine *Household Words* reported: 'A whole family, with some friends, numbering altogether sixteen persons, were *poisoned* lately at Bishop's

Sutton, in Somersetshire, by eating pancakes which had
accidentally been made with an ounce of white arsenic,
sold by mistake for carbonate of soda, which was to have
been used for lightening the pancakes. Medical assistance
was obtained before it was too late, and fortunately no lives
were lost.' This type of accidental poisoning happened in
households all too frequently, partly because there were so
few servants who had received enough education to be able
to read and write anything but the most basic words, and
partly because the least well-educated and well-paid usually
worked at the most lowly jobs in the kitchen, such as laying
out the ingredients for the cook.

In the 1850s, a grand banquet was held for the Irish
Regiment in London. The elaborate table decorations
included precisely rendered green leaves made out of
sugar. Many of the guests were so enchanted by the sugary
decorations that they took them home for their children;
tragically, the leaves had been coloured with Scheele's
green, which proved fatal to several children. Food was
frequently coloured with this poisonous pigment: it was
recorded in pastries and cakes, blancmanges, jellies and
cake icing.

On 11 February 1860, the medical journal *The Lancet*
published an article titled 'Domestic Arsenical Poisoning',
detailing the prevalence of arsenic in the home:

A man may really now-a-days be surrounded with arsenical preparations unawares. There he sits, unconscious in his library, on a summer day, his walls coated with arsenic, a suspicious green dust on his books, and arsenical particles floating in the air, filling his air-passages, inflaming his eyes, disturbing his digestion, and preparing him for dismal and racking pains. He lights a green taper to seal a letter, and as he blows it out he perceives a strong odour, as of onions ... in one form or another [arsenic] haunts us in our walls, in our paper, and paints; it fills the air, and at times gets into our food, poisons our bread, or ... adds fatal charm to our 'Bath buns'.

The passing reference to Bath buns alludes to a story from 1859. The *Inverness Courier* reported on the fatal poisoning in Bristol of 'several persons', including six boarding-school boys, who had all unwittingly eaten Bath buns laced with arsenic. The buns 'were not, as the confectioner supposed, coloured with chromate of lead, but he himself had been deceived by the druggist, who supplied him sulphide of arsenic, a deadly poison, under the false name of the slower poison. The druggist's stock of the sulphide in his shop actually bore a false label.' The fact that chromate of lead was considered an acceptable baking ingredient demonstrates the toxicity of ordinary Victorian cuisine.

LEFT *'This is my appearance after a good dose of ARSENIC taken medicinally.'*
In this British cartoon dating from the 1850s, the skeletal figure of Death appears from behind a screen to observe a patient suffering the adverse effects of arsenic treatment.

In October 1862, the *Manchester Times* reported on the inquest into the death of fifteen-year-old Elizabeth Abdela, from Shoreditch, east London. She had been given a present of artificial grapes, which were painted green, and had sucked some of the colouring. The report by Dr Letheby, professor of chemistry and toxicology from the London Hospital, concluded: 'The green grapes were covered with arsenical green (arsenite of copper) ... The artificial leaves are also stained with arsenical green. Each leaf contains about a grain and a half of the poisonous pigment ... The quantity of poison in one leaf is perhaps sufficient to kill a child.'

The kitchen was not the only area of the Victorian home that harboured lethal amounts of arsenic. In 1862, Leech returned to his earlier theme, with a cartoon entitled 'The Arsenic Waltz. The New Dance of Death (Dedicated to the Green Wreath and Dress-Mongers)'. This satirized the well-publicized use of arsenic to dye clothing textiles and accessories, exacerbated both by the popularity of green clothing and by the trend for women to decorate their hair with wreaths of artificial leaves, which were known to be coloured with arsenical pigments. The *Fife Herald* reported:

> *Arsenical green is employed for the purpose of colouring paper-hangings, tarlatanes for ball dresses, artificial flowers, and other materials of a like nature. Chemically, it is composed of what is popularly known as 'arsenic'*

THE ARSENIC WALTZ.

THE NEW DANCE OF DEATH. (DEDICATED TO THE GREEN WREATH AND DRESS-MONGERS.)

OPPOSITE *The fashionable clothing worn by customers at this American wallpaper shop, c. 1825–36, might have contained as much arsenic as the wallpapers on offer.*

ABOVE *'The Arsenic Waltz' (1862), by* Punch *cartoonist John Leech, depicts the high price of wearing arsenic-dyed fashion: literally, dancing with death.*

(Strictly, arsenious acid, or the white oxide of arsenic). Two-thirds of the whole compositions, therefore, consist of as most virulent poison, between four and five grains of which will kill a human being; and the mixture is laid on so thickly that every lady who wears a dress coloured with emerald green, whisks about on her fair person quite enough to poison between forty and fifty of her fellow-creatures ...

In 1884, the Massachusetts State Board of Health, Lunacy and Charity noted in its annual report that a dress a made from arsenic-green tarlatan might shed twenty to thirty grains of poisonous pigment in just one hour of dancing. With relief, the report revealed that 'Attention has very frequently been called to the presence of large amounts of arsenic in green tarlatan, which has given rise so many times to dangerous symptoms of poisoning when made into dresses and worn, so that it is very rare now to see a green tarlatan dress.'

Of course, those who made the toxic dresses and accessories were exposed to arsenic for much longer periods. By 1859, Ange-Gabriel-Maxime Vernois, a consulting physician, became concerned enough about the effects of arsenic on factory workers to conduct his own independent survey in French workshops where artificial flowers were handmade into bouquets or leaves. Among the symptoms he noted in the (mostly female) workers were 'nausea, colic and diarrhoea, anaemia, pallor and constant headaches that made them feel as if their temples were being pressed in a vice'. Soon thereafter, legislation was passed in both France and Germany to improve working practices in these factories.

The crisis became something of a cause célèbre in Britain when one particular case came to public attention. On 30 November 1861, the London daily newspaper *The Examiner* reported:

> *Fashion has found another victim in the person of a fine girl, named Matilda Scheurer, aged nineteen, whose death, the subject of an inquest, arose from the inhalation of the arsenite of copper employed in colouring the leaves of the artificial flowers of which she was a maker, in the establishment of a M. Bergerond, of Judd Street, Brunswick square ... She had been ill several times before, and complained of pains in the stomach and sickness for the last year and a half. The leaves of the flowers on which she worked were made of wax, and, while wet, emerald green powder was sprinkled upon them ... The post-mortem examination found arsenite of copper in various parts of the body ... A sister of the deceased had died under the same circumstances.*

The factory owner had subsequently given his workers masks, but working conditions had been so hot that it proved difficult to breathe when wearing them. Instead, the girls and women wore muslin over their mouths in a futile attempt to protect themselves. The workers could

LE FOLLET

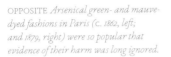

not afford to give up their poorly paid jobs, even though they were exposing themselves to arsenic poisoning every day.

A report commissioned by the Home Office following Matilda Scheurer's death was reported in the *London Evening Standard* in 1863, along with the reminder that 'it is in the power of the public to abstain from articles coloured with emerald green. Ladies may remember that they are, when used as wreaths, or as articles of dress, not only deleterious to themselves, but that they are wrung out of the necessaries, and manufactured out of the flesh and blood, of their own sex.' Despite such heart-rending stories, people continued to clamour for the most vivid greens that artifice could produce and ignored the plight of the factory workers. The following year, another court case concerning the death of a teenager provoked this comment from expert witness Dr Letheby: 'A wreath of fifty green leaves may contain poison enough to kill 100 persons; and a green tarlatan dress of 20 yards would contain about 900 grains of white arsenic; and considering how loosely the poison is attached, it is marvellous that very serious results do not often occur from it.'

American chemist Robert Kedzie voiced similar concerns. He chaired a committee appointed by the Michigan State Board of Health to investigate the dangers of poisons used in everyday life, and delivered a damning report, 'Poisonous Papers', in 1874. Kedzie detailed a case in which a professor at a local college had brought home a case

of lead pencils packaged with a broad band of green paper. His children were attracted to the paper's striking hue and wanted to play with it, but the suspicious professor passed it to Kedzie for analysis first. 'I found it contained enough arsenic to poison all of them,' Kedzie noted, adding that he had also analysed store price tags, paper wrapping for a baby's toy box, postal service packaging and green mail labels, and had found traces of arsenic in every one.

At the beginning of the twentieth century, panic erupted over a new scandal: arsenic in beer. In 1900, one British newspaper published a harrowing story: '[Our] Leeds correspondent learns today that at a large brewery within 16 miles of that city nearly the whole of the employees have been down with a mysterious disease believed to be arsenic poisoning, and it is attributed to the use of some German glucose.' During a four-month period, doctors in the north-west of England were visited by a considerable number of men and women who were suffering from skin discolouration, mutations to finger- and toenails, and limb paralysis. All were discovered to be beer drinkers. The doctors were mystified. Although some patients drank large amounts of beer, many others, who were equally afflicted, drank only moderately. Moreover, heavy drinkers of spirits, such as the whisky-imbibing residents of Glasgow, consumed much higher volumes of alcohol, yet had not suffered the same debilitating symptoms. Pioneering medical breakthroughs finally identified the symptoms as being signs of 'arsenical neuritis', and questions began to be asked about the beer-brewing process and its ingredients.

Despite the newspaper's concerns about 'German' sugar, eventually the problem was traced to the Liverpool-based sugar refinery Bostock & Company. It emerged that, in a drive to produce cut-price sugar, the company had used iron sulphide to make the sulphuric acid that was required to extract the sugar from the cane. Arsenic, often present in iron sulphides, had transferred to the sugar during the separation process. It was discovered that all those afflicted with 'arsenical neuritis' had drunk the cheapest types of beer, brewed with sugar obtained by this method. More expensive beers did not contain arsenic, which is why the wealthier beer-drinking population had not been affected by the poison. Once Bostock & Company's involvement was made public, the furore was so great that the firm was forced to close.

That same year, *The Lancet* reported test results confirming that whisky did not contain arsenic. Sales of whisky rapidly increased, while those of beer plummeted. Finally, in 1903, a Royal Commission report recommended safe levels of arsenic for food and drinks. Unfortunately, its remit did not extend to paint or wallpaper.

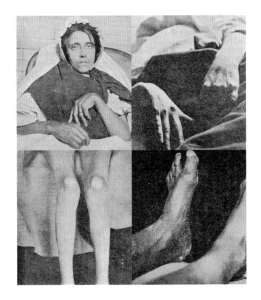

RIGHT *Even light drinkers of cheap beer exhibited grave symptoms in the British arsenical beer poisoning scandal of 1900: 'peripheral neuritis', or inflammation of the nerves, caused muscle paralysis, wasting and loss of sensation. The victims' skin was also affected by keratosis (horny growths), hyperpigmentation and erythema (reddening), as seen on the feet shown bottom right.*

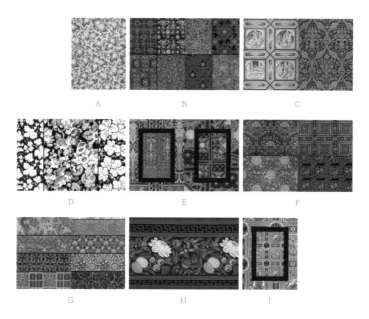

A   B   C

D   E   F

G   H   I

A   I. *** *Yellow/brown, green.* Corbière, Son & Brindle, London, 1877

B   I. ** *Cream/pale brown.* Jeffrey & Company, London, 1880 | 2. *** *Light brown, yellow.* William Cooke, Leeds, UK, 1880 | 3. *** *Pale green, dark green, black.* Ibid., 1880 4. *** *Brown.* Lightbown, Aspinall & Company, London, 1881 | 5.** *Orange/brown.* Ibid., 1881 | 6. ** *Dark green.* William Cooke, Leeds, UK, 1880 | 7. *** *Light brown, yellow.* Ibid., 1880 | 8. ** *Dark green, brown.* Jeffrey & Company, London, 1880

C   I. *** *Yellow, umber red.* Jules Desfossé, Paris, France, 1880 | 2. ** *Green, brown, metallic gold.* Ibid., 1879

D   I. *** *Brown.* C. E. & J. G. Potter, Lancashire, UK, 1856 | 2. *** *Dark brown.* Ibid., 1857 | 3. *** *Green.* Mitchell & Hammond, Manchester, UK, 1856 | 4. *** *Green.* C. E. & J. G. Potter, Lancashire, UK, 1856

E   I. *** *Green.* Jules Desfossé, Paris, France, 1878 | 2. *** *Yellow, brown, dark brown.* Christopher Dresser for William Cooke, Leeds, UK, 1879

F   I. *** *Mid brown.* William Cooke, Leeds, UK, 1881 | 2. *** *Green, black.* Ibid., 1881 3. *** *Green, yellow.* Ibid., 1880 | 4. ** *Brown.* Ibid., 1880

G   I. *** *Brown, green.* William Cooke, Leeds, UK, 1881 | 2. ** *Dark green.* Ibid., 1880 3. *** *Dark brown.* Christopher Dresser for William Woollams & Company, London, 1863 | 4. ** *Olive.* Christopher Dresser for William Cooke, Leeds, UK, 1881 5. *** *Dark green.* William Cooke, Leeds, UK, 1880 | 6. *** *Light brown.* Christopher Dresser for William Cooke, Leeds, UK, 1879 | 7. ** *Dark green.* Charles Knowles & Company, London, 1880 | 8. ** *Yellow, dark green, brown.* Jules Desfossé, Paris, France, 1880

H   I. ** *Dark green.* Corbière, Son & Brindle, London, 1879

I   I. *** *Brown, yellow.* Jules Desfossé, Paris, France, 1879

TOXICITY OF PAPERS: * POSSIBLE   ** PROBABLE   *** HIGHLY LIKELY

CHAPTER FOUR

The Wallpaper Designers

y the late eighteenth century, the French wallpaper industry, concentrated in Paris, had established an enviable reputation and a distinctive style. Floral motifs gained prominence, particularly in the form of large flower vases incorporated into arabesque designs. The appeal of *trompe l'oeil* papers that gave the illusion of fabrics or drapery arose in the late eighteenth century and endured until the 1830s. Allegorical figures and scenes also proved popular subjects.

In France, a panoramic woodblock-printed wallpaper depicting the voyages of Captain Cook, designed in 1804 by Jean-Gabriel Charvet (1750–1829) for Joseph Dufour & Cie, was the first of many large-scale scenic and *trompe l'oeil* wallpapers made by French companies, including Zuber & Cie and Arthur et Robert. Typically, these depicted scenes from nature, complementing the contemporary surge of interest in landscape painting; indeed, early on, they were dubbed *papiers peints-paysages*, or 'landscape wallpapers'. Such projects provided the opportunity to show off the craft and skills of the manufacturers – hundreds of printing blocks might be involved in their creation – and had something of the air of high art about them. One of their distinguishing characteristics was that they did not repeat, as other wallpapers did, each section of the paper. They became popular both at home and abroad, especially in North America, despite their high cost. Perhaps surprisingly, scenic wallpapers survived the subsequent revolution in manufacturing technology and were still

LEFT *This 'scenic wallpaper' in the Renaissance Revival style, issued in 1897 by French company Maison Barbedienne, imitates antique tapestries of bucolic landscapes.*

ABOVE *'Le Paysage à Chasses' (The Hunting Landscape) (1831), a triptych of wallpaper panels manufactured by Zuber & Cie in Rixheim, France.*

ABOVE *A pair of large framed wallpaper panels. This exotic chinoiserie style was the height of fashion in Europe in the eighteenth and nineteenth centuries.*

valued well into the nineteenth century. A set of wallpapers titled the 'Grande Chasse', produced by Eugène Délicourt and displayed at London's Great Exhibition in 1851, were declared 'the moſt remarkable works in the Exhibition' by the French commission.

Pre-eminent among French wallpaper manufaĉturers were Jules Desfossé (1816–1889) and the firms Joseph Dufour & Cie and Zuber & Cie (both founded in 1797), both of whom created speĉtacular *trompe l'oeil* designs and panoramas. Hand-printing dominated in France until 1850, when Zuber & Cie imported the firſt ſteam-powered machine from England. Thereafter, the economic advantages of mechanization proved irresiſtible. By the 1880s, Jean Zuber had calculated that a twenty-colour machine could, in one day, produce an amount of wallpaper that would take a hand-block printer four years to make. The price of a roll of paper plunged from a few gold francs to around 15 centimes. Even so, block-printing and hand-embossed work lived on, right up until 1914, in the market for luxury wallpapers.

French firms also excelled at producing papers that imitated tapeſtries, heightening the effeĉt with embossing and the printing of fine lines to create the illusion of fabric. Paul Balin (1832–1898) was the maſter of embossed wallpapers. He had trained with Desfossé before taking over the Parisian firm Genoux & Cie in 1863, where he began to create faſtidious imitations of hiſtorical textiles and embossed leathers. It was highly specialized work, requiring a large workforce, and Balin's cuſtomers paid for it: juſt one metre

of one of his papers might cost ten gold francs. Nevertheless, sales were healthy, both to decorative arts collections and private connoisseurs, especially in the United States and Britain. The late nineteenth century was truly a golden age for the French wallpaper industry.

By the late 1830s, a growing appreciation in Britain of French wallpapers – with their air of elegance and luxury – resulted in a rise in French imports. Their appeal had spread to the United States, too. In 1800, officials charged with decorating the White House mulled over 'the fitness of pattern, preferring French papers, or second best, those made in England.' To this day, the west side of the Diplomatic Reception Room of the White House is decorated with the panoramic four-panel 'Scenes of North America', designed in 1834 by Zuber & Cie. These renovated panels were installed in 1961 by Jackie Kennedy, along with nineteenth-century wallpapers depicting battle scenes from the American Revolution. The repeal of paper duty in Britain in 1861 only escalated the appetite for French wallpapers.

British wallpapers had reached their zenith in the eighteenth century. Combining skilled block-printing on joined sheets with imaginative and innovate designs, British wallpaper manufacture was then so highly esteemed that the French court started to substitute its tapestries

with British wallpapers. Flocked papers and other *papiers d'Angleterre* were considered so fashionable that spies were employed to find out how they were manufactured. The basic technique involved block-printing designs, using a coloured adhesive, onto a hand-painted background colour. Wool that had been dyed and chopped would then be sprinkled on top for a flock effect; for 'lustre papers', the sprinklings were made of powdered mica, a silicate mineral. The result was startlingly vivid hues and textures, shown to their best advantage by candlelight. By the early nineteenth century, however, British wallpapers were regarded as very much subordinate to their French cousins. Mid-century British papers referenced and imitated antique styles. Gothic-style designs depicted ruined landscapes within pointed arches, while Renaissance motifs, including imitation scrollwork and mock plaster effects, were also prevalent. These designs proved popular with the public, but less so with critics.

By 1837, the British government felt forced to intervene. The state financed new schools of design to train artists to work in the industry; during the following decade, it paid for a string of exhibitions that, it was hoped, would educate the public in the mysteries of good taste. Success was limited, at best: a select committee report in 1849 revealed that British wallpaper companies continued to copy their French counterparts. This fact was underlined by the dominance of French companies at the Great Exhibition of 1851, where Délicourt of Paris won the greatest prizes. The tide began to turn with a mid-century campaign for design reform, driven by painter Richard Redgrave (1804–1888), designer Owen Jones (1809–1874) and civil servant Henry Cole (1808–1882). The group rejected the contemporary appetite for design excess and Redgrave railed against the Rococo revival: 'florid and gaudy compositions, consisting of architectural ornament in relief, with imitative flowers and foliage'. Instead, flat representations and geometric ornamentation were considered exemplary.

Jones made his name not only as a designer and architect, but also as an important theorist and commentator on interior design. He had become well known by his display at the Great Exhibition, and in 1856 his book *The Grammar of Ornament* was in great demand. Much of Jones's inspiration came from Islamic art, and he was a pivotal figure in what became known as the Orientalist movement. In terms of enduring influence, his papers (for high-end firms such as Jeffrey & Company – which advertised itself as a provider of 'Artistic Wallpapers' – and Townsend, Parker & Company, among others) reached their apogee in the use of abstract

LEFT *The frontispiece from* The Grammar of Ornament *(1856) by Owen Jones exemplifies his liberal design philosophy, with Greek keys, medieval manuscript lettering, Celtic interlacing and Islamic ribbed motifs.*

OPPOSITE *Plates from* The Grammar of Ornament. *Jones sought to invigorate British design – not least that of the wallpaper industry that had so fallen behind that of France – by collating patterns from other cultures and disciplines in vibrant colour.*

forms, such as stars and triangles, in primary colours, drawing heavily on Egyptian and Arabic motifs.

At the International Exhibition in London in 1862, British wallpapers were, at long last, lauded and won most of the prizes, while French papers were criticized for their over-elaboration and illusionism. French wallpaper companies were humiliated further when British firms also took home many of the prizes from the Exposition Universelle in Paris in 1867. For its main exhibit, Jeffrey & Company showcased a pilaster decoration designed by Jones, which won a gold medal. A writer for *The Builder* magazine applauded its 'sober, conventional treatments of foliage, exhibiting considerable skill in design and arrangement ... well adapted for backgrounds in rooms of every description'. It was a measure of the growing respect and admiration commanded by contemporary British wallpapers that they were shown at the Fine Arts Exhibition at London's Albert Hall for the first time in 1873.

By the late nineteenth century, companies in the United States – hitherto influenced by floral French designs – were warming to the new British designs. However, manufacturers in the United States were confident that their own products would find a market in Britain. This was partly because – as noted in a report in the London trade magazine *The Furniture Gazette* in 1876 – they would 'strive by their superior mechanical skill to make papers in those designs a little cheaper than their rivals'. Certainly, there was a demand for affordable papers. As *The Furniture Gazette*

observed in 1879, households in the United States
were buying some 57 million rolls of wallpaper per year –
'sufficient to girdle the Earth at the equator and leave
several hundred yards to spare'. The patterns of British
designers William Morris, Christopher Dresser (1834–1904)
and their ilk were emulated widely by artists across the
Atlantic – 'at not more than one-third the price of the no
better papers from England', sniffed *Carpentry and Building*
in 1884. Perhaps influenced by Dresser, the American design
team Associated Artists – comprising Louis Comfort Tiffany
(1848–1933), Candace Wheeler (1827–1923), Lockwood de
Forest (1850–1932) and Samuel Colman (1832–1920) – produced
Japanese and Indian-style patterns for New York firm
Warren, Fuller & Company.

Dresser was among the most highly praised wallpaper
designers of the time. Along with Jones, he was one of
the earliest ornamentalists to be involved with the South
Kensington Museum (now called the Victoria and Albert
Museum) in London, and many of his designs were informed
by the treasures that it housed. Another key influence
was a journey that he made through Japan in the mid 1870s.
The Orientalist and Aesthetic artistic movements were at
their height, and Japanese art, clothing and decor played

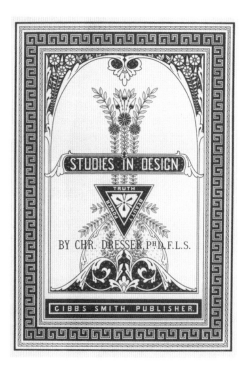

LEFT *Frontispiece
of* Studies in Design
*(1876) by British
designer Christopher
Dresser. Dresser's
aim was 'to bring
about a better style
of decoration for
our houses'.*

OPPOSITE *Colour
plates from* Studies in
Design, *with Eastern,
North African,
natural and geometric
motifs. Dresser's
interpretations of
organic forms and
historical patterns
anticipate the Art
Nouveau movement
by some three decades.*

a key role in both. Japan had been closed off from the outside world for more than two centuries, ever since the country's *sakoku* 'isolation policy' had begun in 1635. In 1853, American naval commander Commodore Matthew Perry had sailed into Tokyo harbour and demanded that the Japanese sign a trade and shipping agreement with the United States. As the Japanese had no navy – their isolation meant they had not needed one – they had little choice, and in 1854 Japan reluctantly opened up to trade.

Japanese art, textiles and designs quickly became prized in the Western world and Japonism was born. Aesthetic artists became as obsessed with Japanese art as their predecessors had been with Chinese art, and thousands of customers aspired to import such fashionable exoticism into their homes. One popular import was Japanese leather paper: a very thick and expensive type of embossed wallpaper with a texture that resembled finely tanned leather. The paper was debuted at the London International Exhibition of 1862; Dresser went on to be one of the first interior designers to use it. In 1879, he set up a new company, Dresser & Holmes, specializing in selling Japanese goods to Britain and the United States. He was perceived as a leading arbiter of decorative taste in Britain. In his book *Studies in Design* (1876), Dresser complains about householders who tell decorators how they wish their home to look – and about decorators who allow themselves to be influenced by their clients' wishes:

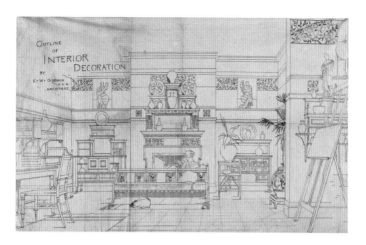

What should we think if, when a medical man is
called to see us, he asked how we would like the complaint
treated; what medicine we desire; and if a tonic, whether
we would have bark or arsenic? The decoration of a
room is as much bound by laws and by knowledge as the
treatment of a disease. A surgeon would not cut off an arm
simply because a patient asked him so to do; he would first
ascertain whether it was curable. I have no knowledge
of the treatment of the diseases; hence I commit myself
to the care of a physician. I have no understanding of
law; hence I employ a solicitor. I am called in to decorate
a room; my client is as ignorant of my art as I am of him.
Is it not my duty, then, to tell him that the room would look
well if treated in such a way; or that its walls might be of
such a colour? If we have understanding of our art, it is
easy to convince others, who are ignorant, that we have
more knowledge of the subject than they have; but we must
be able to show a reason for the suggestions that we make.

British decorative arts designers led the world in the mid-
nineteenth century. Edward Godwin (1833–1886) was an early
exponent of Aesthetic design. In addition to wallpapers,
he designed artist James Abbott McNeill Whistler's White
House in Chelsea and a garden studio at Kensington Palace
for Princess Louise, Queen Victoria's daughter. In the mid-
1860s, Bruce Talbert (1838–1881), a well-known architect and
designer of furniture and wallpaper, left his native Scotland

for London and embraced the spirit of Aestheticism. He wrote three books, which were popular in both Britain and the United States. Talbert died at the age of forty-three, but had managed to create a prodigious body of work. Like Dresser, he believed in decorating to his own specifications, rather than those of the owner.

Charles Francis Annesley Voysey (1857–1941) was also an architect and a designer of wallpaper and textiles. His belief was that every home should be a unique work of art, entire in itself. A member of Morris's Arts and Crafts Movement, Voysey incorporated nature into most of his designs, finding inspiration in native British flora and fauna. German critic Hermann Muthesius praised Voysey, noting, '[He] adheres more closely to Morris's more primitive plant designs and likes to combine birds with plant forms. His colours are deeper and richer than Crane's and altogether one can say that he is the one who has best continued Morris's great tradition.'

Edward Burne-Jones (1833–1898) became one of the best-known Pre-Raphaelite artists and designers of the second half of the nineteenth century, working with his close friend Morris to create textiles, stained glass and legendary wallpapers. A founding partner of the firm that launched Morris's business career, Morris, Marshall, Faulkner & Company, he continued to work with Morris on designs and illustrations for textiles and wallpapers, alongside his own large-scale paintings.

Working closely with manufacturers, Lewis Foreman Day (1845–1910) embraced the latest technologies. He was a prominent member of the Arts and Crafts Movement

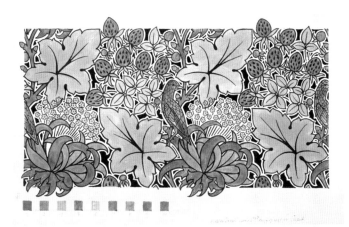

and the Aesthetic and Art Nouveau communities. He was
one of the best-known British wallpaper designers of his
era, renowned for his innovative patterns and use of colour.

Walter Crane (1845–1915) completed his first wallpaper
design in 1874 and was soon recognized as a talent to
be nurtured. He became one of the favoured designers
of Jeffrey & Company (which took on the production
of more than sixty of Morris's patterns after the designer
found himself struggling to manufacture them all) and was
the first president of the Arts and Crafts Exhibition Society.
Crane worked closely with many of the best-known designers
and artists of the day, including Morris and Frederic, Lord
Leighton. Muthesius was full of admiration for him:
'Walter Crane with his characteristic versatility introduces
new motifs, especially figural and animal, into wallpaper,
[he] borrows freely, now from the antique repertoire of
forms, now from the medieval, uses his own individual
lines and colours and is almost inexhaustible in the
imaginativeness of his design.'

The most renowned designer of the late nineteenth
century is undoubtedly William Morris. He drew acclaim
not only for his designs, but also for his connection with
the Pre-Raphaelite movement, his marriage to Jane Burden
(one of the Pre-Raphaelites' favoured models), his socialism
and his philanthropic campaigns. Fervently against mass
production, Morris spearheaded the Arts and Crafts

Movement, joining forces in 1861 with Burne-Jones, Ford Madox Brown, Charles Faulkner, Dante Rossetti, Peter Paul Marshall and Philip Webb to set up Morris, Marshall, Faulkner & Company: 'Fine Art Workmen in Painting, Carving, Furniture and the Metals'. The company's medieval-inspired designs were an immediate hit at the International Exhibition of 1862.

Morris designed most of the company's tapestries and forty-one of its wallpapers. His designs were inspired by nature, featuring motifs of flowers, stems, leaves, fruit and birds arranged in dynamic patterns filled with movement. He held that in wallpaper design 'the aim should be to combine clearness of form and firmness of structure with the mystery which comes from abundance and richness of detail'. All of his designs were hand-printed, one colour at a time, using pear-wood blocks made by craftsmen at Jeffrey & Company in Islington, London. The designs were traced onto blocks, which were then painstakingly cut into the wood, under Morris's supervision. Thanks to the popularity of his work, the designer's name became synonymous with wallpaper.

Like many of his contemporaries, most of Morris's well-known early designs contained arsenic-based colours, including his popular Daisy, Fruit, Trellis, Venetian, Scroll and Larkspur patterns. Moreover (as discussed in Chapter Two) he had inherited his wealth from the profits of his

LEFT *Samples of William Morris's wallpaper designs, from his firm's output maintained by Jeffrey & Company of London. The samples are pasted into a Jeffrey & Company accounts book.*

father's shares in a highly lucrative British arsenic mine called Devon Great Consols. Like most Victorians, Morris seems to have believed that arsenic in design pigments differed in some way from the poison that often made the headlines. In 1874, he dissolved Morris, Marshall, Faulkner & Company, which allowed him to set up Morris & Company in 1875 under his sole ownership. The same year, he resigned from Devon Great Consols and sold his shares two years later. At this point, Morris turned his attention to dyeing methods, calling for a return to using old-fashioned vegetable dyes to obtain more delicate, less crude colours. In 1881, the success of the weaving, dyeing and cotton-printing part of the business led Morris to move the workshops from cramped conditions in Queen Square, London, to Merton Abbey Mills, the site of a medieval abbey and an eighteenth-century textile factory near Morden in north Surrey, alongside the tree-lined banks of the River Wandle. The river water was perfect for use in the dyeing process and the wooden sheds were turned into a dye house, glass-painting studio, printing shop and weaving factory. Here, Morris created excellent working conditions for his labourers and paid fair wages, putting into practice the egalitarian beliefs that he espoused.

By the end of the nineteenth century, those who could afford it were papering their homes liberally with a plethora of different wallpapers. It became fashionable to paste new wallpaper over old-fashioned oak panelling, and to feature clashing colours and themes on the walls of the same room. In his book *The English House* (1904–05), Muthesius wrote scathingly of the Victorian obsession with wallpaper, with walls and ceilings 'papered all over ... in old houses where the wooden panelling had survived, the panelling was ripped out of the best rooms and the walls were papered'. Decorators seldom removed existing papers before hanging new ones, so that layer upon layer of papers dyed with numerous toxic pigments were pasted on top of one another.

In an essay published in a book entitled *Our Homes, And How To Make Them Healthy* (1883), British architect Robert W. Edis criticized this practice, stressing the importance of scraping off and washing down walls before putting up new wallpaper, claiming that 'not only does the paste of the old papering often decompose, and become in itself injurious to health, but each covering of paper only adds to the absorbent nature of the walls, and helps to increase therefore the unhealthiness and stuffiness of the room'. He also advised against patterned wallpaper in bedrooms. 'The endless multiplication and monotony of strongly-marked patterns ... [is] a source of infinite torture and annoyance in times of sickness and sleeplessness.' Was he confusing the decorative effect of the patterns with the physical effects of arsenic?

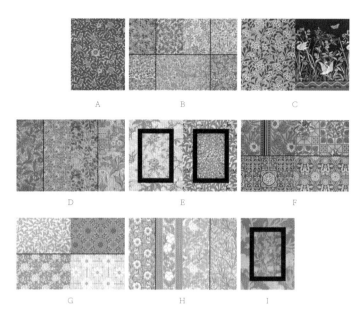

A   B   C

D   E   F

G   H   I

A   1. *** *Brown*. Lightbown, Aspinall & Company, Lancashire, UK, 1881
B   1. ** *Dark green, black*. Lightbown, Aspinall & Company, Lancashire, UK, 1881
     2. *** *Pale yellow/green*. William Cooke, Leeds, UK, 1880 | 3. *** *Pale brown*. Ibid., 1880
     4. ** *Dark green*. Ibid., 1880 | 5. ** *Orange*. Ibid., 1879 | 6. ** *Pink, brown*. Ibid., 1879
     7. *** *Yellow green*. Ibid., 1881 | 8. *** *Green/brown*. Ibid., 1881
C   1. *** *Yellow/brown, metallic gold*. William Cooke, Leeds, UK, 1881
     2. ** *Pale green*. Corbière, Son & Brindle, London, UK, 1879
D   1. *** *Dark green*. Lightbown, Aspinall & Company, Lancashire, UK, 1881
     2. ** *Yellow, green*. William Cooke, Leeds, UK, 1881 | 3. *** *Yellow/brown*.
     Lightbown, Aspinall & Company, Lancashire, UK, 1881 | 4. *** *Peach, pale yellow*
     & brown lines. Corbière, Son & Brindle, London, UK, 1879
E   1. *** *Yellow, dark green, brown*. Jules Desfossé, Paris, France, 1879
     2. *** *Yellow, brown*. William Cooke, Leeds, UK, 1881
F   1. *** *Yellow*. Lightbown, Aspinall & Company, Lancashire, UK, 1880
     2. *** *Light green*. William Cooke, Leeds, UK, 1878 | 3. *** *Yellow, green, black*.
     Ibid., 1879
     4. *** *Green, brown*. Ibid., 1878
G   1. *** *Yellow, pink, brown*. Charles Knowles & Company, London, UK, 1880
     2. ** *Dark green*. William Cooke, Leeds, UK, 1880 | 3. *** *Dark green, black, lighter*
     green. Lightbown, Aspinall & Company, Lancashire, UK, 1881 | 4. ** *Pale pink*.
     William Cooke, Leeds, UK, 1879
H   1. *** *Yellow, brown, beige*. William Cooke, Leeds, UK, 1880 | 2. ** *Yellow, pale yellow,*
     green. Lightbown, Aspinall & Company, Lancashire, UK, 1880 | 3. *** *Yellow*.
     William Cooke, Leeds, UK, 1881 | 4. *** *Yellow, pale yellow*. Lightbown, Aspinall
     & Company, Lancashire, UK, 1881
I   1. *** *Green*. Charles Knowles & Company, London, UK, 1879

TOXICITY OF PAPERS: * POSSIBLE   ** PROBABLE   *** HIGHLY LIKELY

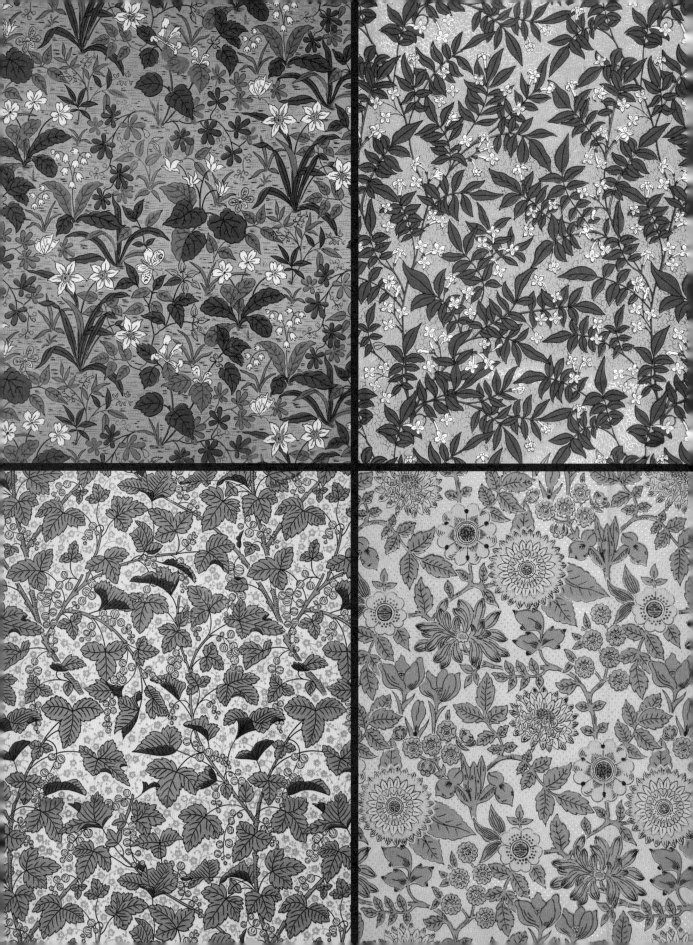

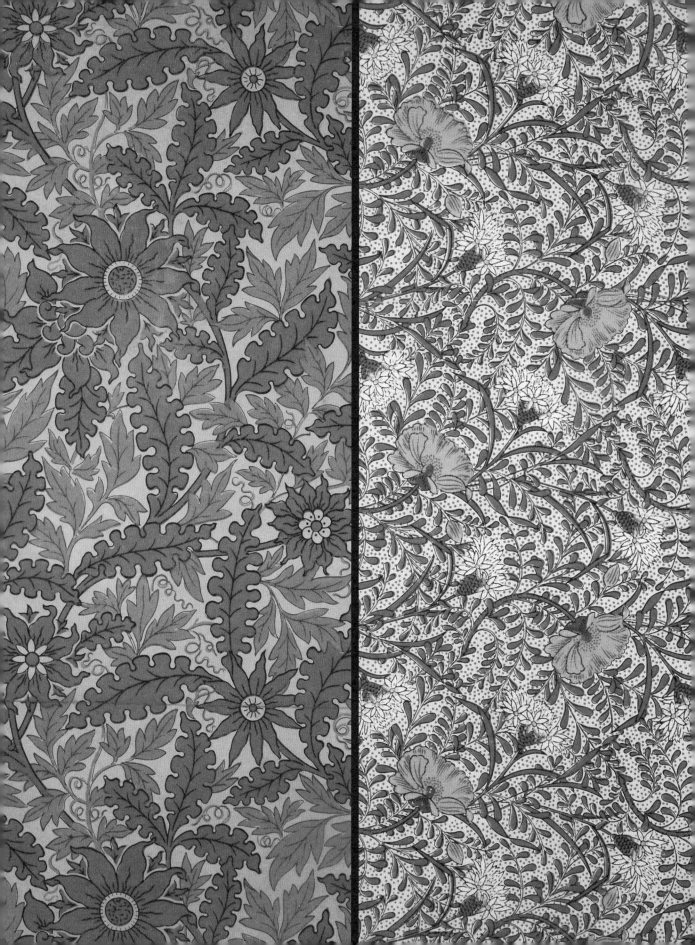

n the 1850s, British social reformer and political activist Harriet Martineau wrote a series of articles about modern industries for Charles Dickens's magazine *Household Words*. In one article she included a story about arsenical wallpaper dust:

> *[The] room was very prettily hung, not long ago, with a paper where a bright green trail of foliage was the most conspicuous part of the pattern. Day after day everything in the room was found covered with a green dust; and the pattern on the wall faded in proportion. The size had, in fact, been insufficient to fix the green powder, one ingredient of which, by the way, was arsenic ...*

The comment about the arsenic was simply an aside; the irritation felt by the householder was not about the toxicity of the wallpaper, but about the expense incurred by having to redecorate the room because the green dust falling from the walls had caused the pattern to fade. Martineau was driving at the importance of interior decorators using proper techniques: in this case, understanding how to prepare the correct formula for 'size' (a liquid used

LEFT *A mother and daughter in a typical Victorian child's bedroom, c. 1890, decorated with what might very well be arsenical wallpaper.*

OPPOSITE *'Is Life Worth Living? Or, The Haunted Householder' (1885). This* Punch *cartoon by Linley Sambourne shows a homeowner assailed by phantom threats, including a devil emerging from wallpaper decorated with skulls and labelled 'arsenic'.*

IS LIFE WORTH LIVING? OR, THE HAUNTED HOUSEHOLDER

to provide a smooth and adherent base). The size, it was
believed, was the aspect of wallpapering that could prove
problematic, as Martineau explained:

> [N]one but the best size should be used for attaching the
> paper to the walls. Many a fever has been caused by the
> horrible nuisance of corrupt size used in paper-hanging
> in bed-rooms. The nausea which the sleeper is aware of on
> waking in the morning, in such a case should be a warning
> needing no repetition. Down should come the whole paper
> at any cost or inconvenience; for it is an evil which allows
> of no tampering.

Martineau was a few years too early to realize that stories
such as hers would have great importance in the future,
and would become the subject of intense speculation
by newspapers about the use of arsenic in wallpaper.
　　The first reports of wallpaper poisoning appeared
in the late 1850s, initially in medical literature and letters
submitted to the national press by doctors. In February
1857, Birmingham doctor William Hinds wrote an article
in the *Medical Times and Gazette*, describing the sickness
he had experienced after redecorating his study with
a green-tinged wallpaper. 'A great deal of slow poisoning

LEFT *This green-papered 'Aesthetic interior' showcases works by British Arts and Crafts designers William Morris and William De Morgan (1839-1917). Morris refused to believe that his arsenical wallpapers were dangerous.*

LEFT *Nineteenth-century watercolour showing a day room decorated with fashionable green wallpaper and a border with a foliage design. Chemists and doctors began to caution the public about the dangers of green wallpaper in the 1850s.*

LEFT *This British interior, c. 1870s, is papered in the latest style, with floral and classical patterns on a green background, very likely arsenical.*

is going on in Great Britain,' Hinds asserted. Newspapers quickly took up the story of the scandal, although for some time to come it was mistakenly believed that only green pigments contained arsenic. Some of the stories became national news and were picked up by physicians in other countries. Case histories were shared in medical journals and the newspapers gleefully reprinted them, so that stories that would usually have remained confined to the readerships of *The Lancet* and the *British Medical Journal* became hot topics of discussion in drawing rooms, gentlemen's clubs and public houses all over the country. A letter written by a chemist to the editor of the *Morning Post* on 15 June 1859 reiterated the dangers being raised by doctors:

> *Sir, I beg you will accord me a small space in your columns to call the attention of the public to the extreme danger of green paper hangings.*
>
> *I was yesterday consulted by a gentleman who has long suffered from general ill-health. He has had the best medical advice in vain. His physician, finding medicine of no avail, imagined that his patient's ailments might be occasioned by the arsenic in the green papers of his rooms. This afternoon I have analysed three specimens of the paper and some of the dust swept from the floor. In each of the papers I found a great quantity of arsenic and the dust also contained a very large proportion of that fearful poison. I would, therefore, earnestly recommend the public not to paper their rooms with papers containing that colour, and, in cases where rooms are already covered with green, to have the walls well sized and varnished in order to prevent the dust poisoning the atmosphere.*

This missive encapsulated a growing fear, although one ignored by most Victorians. A vocal undercurrent was starting to make itself known in the press, in campaigning committees and in the more enlightened areas of society.

Newspaper and magazine cartoons of the time frequently satirized the laissez-faire attitude to arsenical wallpapers, on the part of both the government and the general public, and the lack of effective legislation against them. Cartoons were powerful tools, not only because publications such as *Punch* (which ran from 1841 in Britain) and *Puck* (a satirical magazine from the United States, first published in 1871) were widely read across all levels of society, but also because they were pored over by politicians, who feared being made to look idiotic in their pages. Campaigning journalism and cartoons helped to bring about the law that restricted the sale of arsenic in Britain in 1851.

In 1869, a novel, published anonymously by one 'Green Englishman', bore the melodramatic title *The Green of the Period; or, The unsuspected foe in the Englishman's home*. It begins at a hotel in Dover, Kent, in which Sir Robert Chichester is asked why he has been unable to settle in one of the rooms, and whether he is fearful of ghosts. His response is emphatic: 'No, it was "death on the walls" that scared me, and I would sooner have betaken myself to the stables than have established my quarters even for one night, in the arsenical den to which they first assigned me.' Once on the boat to France, Chichester assures his friends that many of the countries they are travelling to 'are far more alive than ourselves to the danger'. His friends remain sceptical, until a doctor, travelling on the same boat, relates his own experiences of arsenical wallpaper. Written in an easy-to-read, sensationalized style, the novel was intended to instruct the public without preaching.

HALF-A-CROWN.

The Green of the Period.

LONDON: GEORGE ROUTLEDGE & SONS.

LEFT *The front cover of* The Green of the Period *(1869), a sensational anonymous novel about the dangers of arsenical wallpaper.*

OPPOSITE Shadows from the Walls of Death *(1874) may well be the most dangerous book of all time. It consists of eighty-six pages of arsenical wallpaper samples, assembled by Robert Kedzie, an American chemist who investigated toxic wallpapers for the Michigan state Board of Health.*

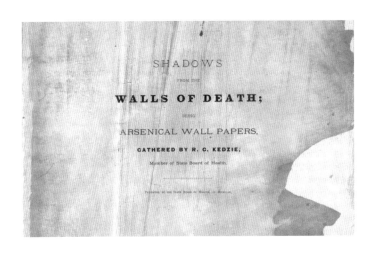

In the United States, chemist Robert Kedzie included
several examples of poisoning by wallpaper in his essay
'Poisonous Papers' (1874) for the Michigan State Board
of Health. As part of a campaign to alert the public to the
dangers of arsenical wallpapers, Kedzie collected wallpaper
samples from stores in Detroit, Lansing and Jackson, and
had them trimmed and bound into one hundred books,
which he distributed to libraries throughout Michigan.
Titled *Shadows from the Walls of Death*, the books proved
a remarkably direct and effective means of publicizing
the dangers of arsenic in wallpaper. Not that the American
wallpaper industry was quick to react: by 1887, the American
Medical Association reported that 54 to 65 per cent of all
wallpaper sold in the United States between 1879 and 1883
contained arsenic – and that a third of that total contained
dangerous levels of the poison.

In London, *The Times* printed scores of hard-hitting
articles about arsenic, keeping stories of human misery and
poisoning in the public eye. In 1875, the newspaper claimed
that the mines of Devon Great Consols alone 'contained
enough arsenic to poison the entire world'. Although the
press was filled with outraged reports of the dangers of
domestic wallpapers and the legions of people who were
being affected by them, noticeably lacking were articles
about the people who produced the wallpapers. In the 1870s,
the Medical Society of London set up a committee to look
into the problems of arsenical wallpaper. The chairman,
Jabez Hogg, noted: 'In the course of a few weeks no less
than fifty-four reports of cases reached me of arsenic
poisoning by wallpapers.' The committee was disappointed

by the lack of attention paid to the problem by the medical community. It also attempted to lobby artists and wallpaper manufacturers, but only three agreed to take part (and they had all already switched to using non-arsenical pigments).

The report also brought to the attention of the public the news that green was not the only pigment colour to contain arsenic. In 1880, the *Exeter and Plymouth Gazette* reported:

> It is generally believed that bright greens are the most arsenical, and it is a fact that many are very highly so, but at the same time there are other colours equally arsenical which are little suspected, and there are bright greens perfectly harmless in their nature ... It is an indisputable fact, well known to chemists acquainted with the working of paperstainers' factories, that where no restriction is placed on the use of arsenical colours, all the goods made on the premises become more or less contaminated, a dull neutral colour may be as likely to cause mischief as a bright and gaudy one.

In September 1875, the *Leamington Spa Courier* carried a story about the Jones family, who all appeared to be suffering from arsenic poisoning, under the headline: 'Poisoning by Arsenical Wall Paper – not Green'. The wallpapers in the family home were tested, and 'of seven kinds of paper, six were found to contain arsenic'. In fact, the green wallpaper contained considerably less arsenic, prompting new concerns that *all* colours of wallpaper might be toxic.

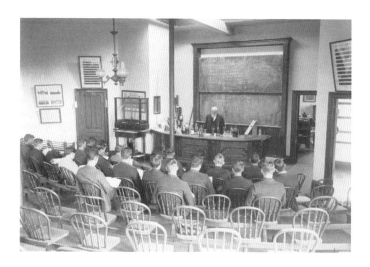

One campaigner on a mission to educate the homeowner was Sir Shirley Foster Murphy, medical officer of health for the Parish of St Pancras, who edited a collection of essays by leading medical journalists and published them in *Our Homes and How to Make Them Healthy* (1883). Explaining how each room should be arranged and used in order to ensure the family's safety, the book also discussed interior decor:

We like to think and act for ourselves, and at first blush it does look as if by discarding arsenic we should deprive ourselves of some of our best colours. But this is not the case. Aestheticism need 'moult no feather', for ... It is well known that the most beautiful and delicate tints can be produced without employing one single grain of arsenic ... Danger is lurking at the present moment unsuspected in many a home, and ... it is no uncommon thing for men and women to die, poisoned by arsenic in a wall-paper.

In his report 'On the Proportion of Arsenic Present in Paper-hangings' (1861), British chemist Dr Stevenson Macadam queried 'whether arsenic volatilized at ordinary temperatures'. He thought it was possible that, after wallpapers were pasted, 'a certain proportion of the arsenic

ABOVE *'The Empty Crib' (1899). Was arsenic in the patterned nursery wallpaper responsible for the infant death mourned in this American stereograph image?*

OPPOSITE *The women in this photograph of a typical Victorian interior, c. 1890–1910, could be surrounded by toxic dyes in their clothing, soft furnishings and wallpaper.*

was carried off with the water in the shape of vapour', although he believed that physical disturbance of the pigments, such as by a maid dusting the wall, or the skirt of a passing woman brushing against the wallpaper, was more likely to cause arsenic poisoning. Consultant Henry Aspland disagreed with Macadam and declared that 'as a medical man' he was 'quite satisfied that arsenic floating in the air could do no harm'. He also made the startling comment that arsenic was 'one of the finest tonics that medical men possessed and the use of it was becoming general – in fact, the taking of it tended to prolong life'. This comment reportedly elicited widespread laughter from the men in the audience, perhaps because of arsenic's reputation as an aphrodisiac.

As the medical profession remained baffled by the inconsistencies of arsenic poisoning, the Medical Society of London released a list of known symptoms. It was divided into four sections: the stomach and bowels; the eyes; the nervous system; and the throat, nose and respiratory organs, with a warning that victims might exhibit all, or only one or two, of the symptoms. Sceptics dismissed the report.

In *The Arsenic Century* (2010), James Whorton relates a story of how wallpaper poisoning affected even the royal family. Allegedly, in 1879, Queen Victoria was kept waiting at Buckingham Palace by the late arrival of one of her guests. When the dignitary finally made his embarrassed appearance, he looked as though he had come from a hospital ward, not from one of the country's most prestigious bedrooms. He had been sleeping in a guest room decorated with green wallpaper and had experienced a terrible night of illness. The queen promptly ordered any arsenical wallpaper to be stripped from the palace's walls.

The *Exeter and Plymouth Gazette* published a long article in 1880 presenting the arguments for and against the dangers of arsenic in wallpaper. Commenting that it had been outlawed in most other household items, it explained:

> *One great reason why the use of arsenical colours in paper hangings … has been so long permitted to remain unchallenged, is the comparative immunity of the workpeople employed in the manufacture which, doubtless, fostered the honest belief, on the part of the manufacturers, that the outcry against the use of arsenic was a mere fad …*

Henry Carr, author of *Our Domestic Poisons* (1883), was passionate about the need for change and challenged the doctors who refused to believe that arsenic could be poisonous, despite using it to kill vermin in their homes. In his introduction, Carr wrote: 'Does not the manufacturer

know perfectly well that the public would not purchase a single piece of his wallpapers, were they marked, "Impregnated with arsenic, a subtle poison, which may diffuse itself for an indefinite period through the air of the room"?' His call for urgent parliamentary action was not answered.

In 1882, newspapers revealed that the British Foreign Office had told its overseas employees to report back 'on the existing legislation in Continental countries with reference to the precautions and restrictions imposed on the manufacture and sale of articles in which arsenical pigments have been employed'. The National Health Society, which had been lobbying the government about arsenic, formed a committee 'to investigate the subject of arsenic poisoning – in respect to ... materials in daily use, and their deleterious effect on health'. Yet the British government stood fast.

Although evidence of wallpaper poisoning was mounting, William Morris was sceptical of the public's fears. In 1885, he wrote to his friend Thomas Wardle:

I cannot imagine it possible that the amount of lead which might be in a paper could give people lead poisoning ... As to the arsenic scare a greater folly it is hardly possible to imagine: the doctors were bitten as people were bitten by the witch fever ... My belief about it all is that doctors find their patients ailing, don't know what's the matter with them, and in despair put it down to the wall papers when they probably ought to put it down to the water closet, which I believe to be the source of all illness.

A few days later, Morris wrote again to Wardle about a current case, and pointed out, 'it is proving too much to prove that the Nicholsons were poisoned by wallpapers: for if they were, a great many other people would be in the same plight and we should be sure to hear about it'.

In the second letter, Morris is somewhat defensive. There had been many recorded 'cases' throughout his career, and it is aſtonishing that he had never worried about the effeᶜt of arsenical colours on the health of his wallpaper labourers. Yet, like many medical specialiſts, he was not alone in believing that some doᶜtors and newspaper editors were on a witch hunt. Morris and Edward Burne-Jones both decorated their homes with Morris & Company's arsenical wallpaper, and neither family, it seems, suffered from any ill effeᶜts. It was not yet recognized by moſt physicians that an identical exposure to arsenic in any given group of people might not have the same effeᶜt on all of them. Moreover, the symptoms of arsenic poisoning were similar to those of multiple illnesses prevalent in the nineteenth century, including those caused by food poisoning.

In the 1880s, scientiſts began to discuss the hypothesis that domeſtic arsenic poisoning might be caused by something other than pigments that fell from wallpaper. A breakthrough came in 1891, when an Italian medical

LEFT *'When Doctors Disagree' (1898) from* Puck *magazine. An elderly doctor with poisons and an 'Old School Drug Cure' sits in front of 'Chockful Cemetery', while a younger man with a 'New School Mind Cure' stands in front of a relatively empty 'Nodrugs Cemetery'.*

OPPOSITE *Frontispiece: 'Thus ornament is but the guilèd shore/ To a most dangerous sea' (left); and an advertisement for Reinsch's test for arsenic (right), from* Our Domestic Poisons *(1879) by Henry Carr.*

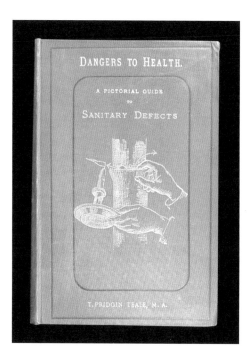

scientist named Bartolomeo Gosio returned to Leopold Gmelin's work on the gas released by arsenical pigments. Gosio examined cases in which poisoning occurred even when no arsenical wallpaper was obviously present and found hidden older layers of toxic papers. His experiments confirmed that it was a gas, notably produced in damp conditions, that made the wallpapers poisonous. Unlike Gmelin, who described the smell as being 'mouse-like', Gosio described it as garlicky. Later, in the 1930s, British chemist Frederick Challenger identified 'Gosio's gas' as trimethylarsine.

One of the most infamous cases of death by wallpaper poisoning involved a family of children in the east London area of Limehouse. On 3 May 1862, newspapers reported the death of Ann Amelia Turner, aged three. Her three siblings had all died before her and, initially, were believed to have contracted diphtheria. When no one else in the community became ill, however, questions were raised. Toxicology expert Dr Letheby was called in, and in due course the deaths were revealed to have been caused by arsenic poisoning. The *British Medical Journal* noted in its article on the court case: 'Large pieces of the paper had been torn down by the children. They had played with portions, and licked the green colour off the surface.' Despite this, and the fact that the judge condemned the use of green wallpaper as 'objectionable', the jury returned a verdict of 'natural death'. The *Reading Mercury* noted: 'The verdict appeared to create great astonishment in the court', while the astounded coroner declared, 'I cannot refrain from expressing my entire dissent from the verdict. The medical evidence not only proves that there was no disease to account for death, but that there were no remains of disease.'

Frequent though cases of wallpaper poisoning were, there were many alternative sources of arsenic in nineteenth-century homes. So ubiquitous was the use of arsenic as a pigment that individuals risked becoming poisoned simply by going about their daily routines. In 1904, the United States Department of Agriculture published a report into arsenic in wallpapers and fabrics. It included the story of a doctor in Boston who suffered from pain in his fingers; his gloves were found to be free of arsenic. Eventually, the toxic pigment was discovered in his pack of coloured playing cards. Another case occurred at a children's home in Massachusetts. The walls and carpets were arsenic-free, but children continued to decline and suffered breathing problems. Two babies died before it was discovered that there was arsenic in the dye of the nurses' blue uniforms. The report also noted that out of four commercially available wallpapers found to have toxic levels of arsenic, 'two of the four samples came from England, one of the foreign countries which has no laws limiting the amount of arsenic in papers and fabrics'. Citizens had little choice but to avoid these products to protect themselves.

Stripping off Poisonous Wall Papers.

PLATE LXVII.

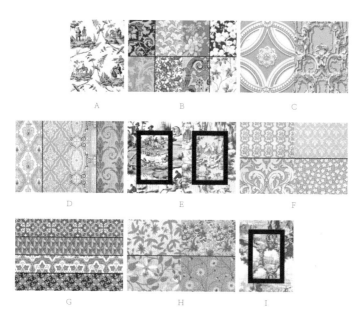

A   1. ••• *Green.* John Todd Merrick & Company, London, UK, 1845

B   1. ••• *Green.* Henry N. Turner & Company, London, UK, 1852 | 2. ••• *Green.* James Toleman, London, UK, 1856 | 3. ••• *Light green.* C. E. & J. G. Potter, Lancashire, UK, 1845 | 4. ••• *Red, light green.* Corbière, Son & Brindle, London, UK, 1877 | 5. ••• *Green.* Scott, Cuthbertson & Company, London, UK, 1856 | 6. ••• *Green.* C. E. & J. G. Potter, Lancashire, UK, 1856 | 7. ••• *Yellow.* Corbière, Son & Brindle, London, UK, 1877 | 8. ••• *Green.* C. E. & J. G. Potter, Lancashire, UK, 1857

C   1. ••• *Green.* Wilcoxon & Sons, London, UK, 1847 | 2. ••• *Light green.* John Todd Merrick & Company, London, UK, 1845

D   1. ••• *Green.* C. E. & J. G. Potter, Lancashire, UK, 1856 | 2. ••• *Green.* Williams, Coopers, Boyle & Company, London, UK, 1856 | 3. ••• *Green.* Wilcoxon & Sons, London, UK, 1845 | 4. ••• *Green.* Pavy's Patent Felted Fabric Company Limited, London, UK, 1873

E   1. ••• *Green.* Trumble & Cooke, Leeds, UK, 1852 | 2. ••• *Dark green.* Elisha Thomas Archer, London, UK, 1852

F   1. ••• *Green.* C. E. & J. G. Potter, Lancashire, UK, 1856 | 2. ••• *Green.* James Boswell, Dublin, Ireland, 1846 | 3. ••• *Green.* Christopher Dresser for William Cooke, Leeds, UK, 1860 | 4. ••• *Green.* C. E. & J. G. Potter, Lancashire, UK, 1856

G   1. ••• *Dark green.* William Woollams & Company, London, UK, 1863 | 2. ••• *Dark green.* Christopher Dresser for William Woollams & Company, London, UK, 1863 | 3. ••• *Green, pink.* Ibid., 1863 | 4. ••• *Green, purple, brown.* Ibid., 1863

H   1. •• *Brown.* William Cooke, Leeds, UK, 1879 | 2. ••• *Green, brown line.* Ibid., 1879 | 3. •• *Yellow/brown/beige, pale yellow.* Ibid., 1880 | 4. ••• *Dark green.* Ibid., 1879

I   1. ••• *Dark green.* Heywood, Higginbottom, Smith & Company, Manchester, UK, 1852

TOXICITY OF PAPERS: • POSSIBLE   •• PROBABLE   ••• HIGHLY LIKELY

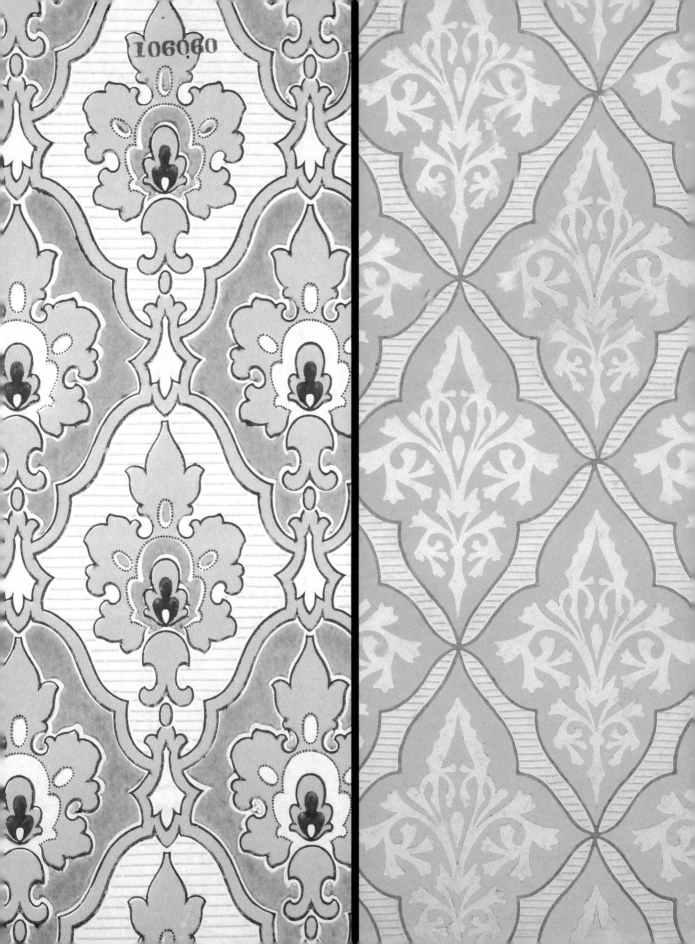

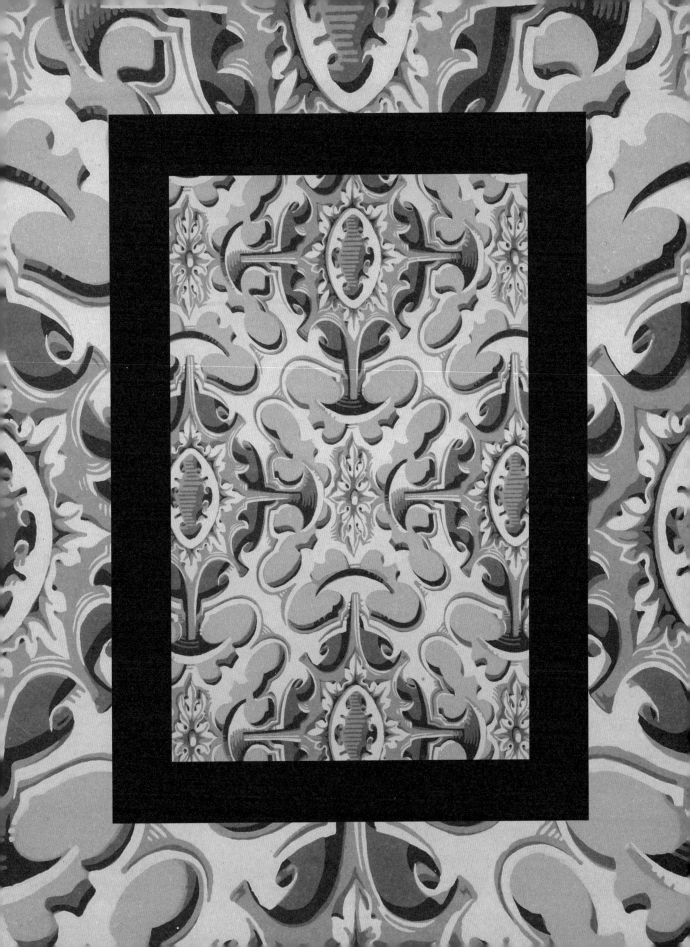

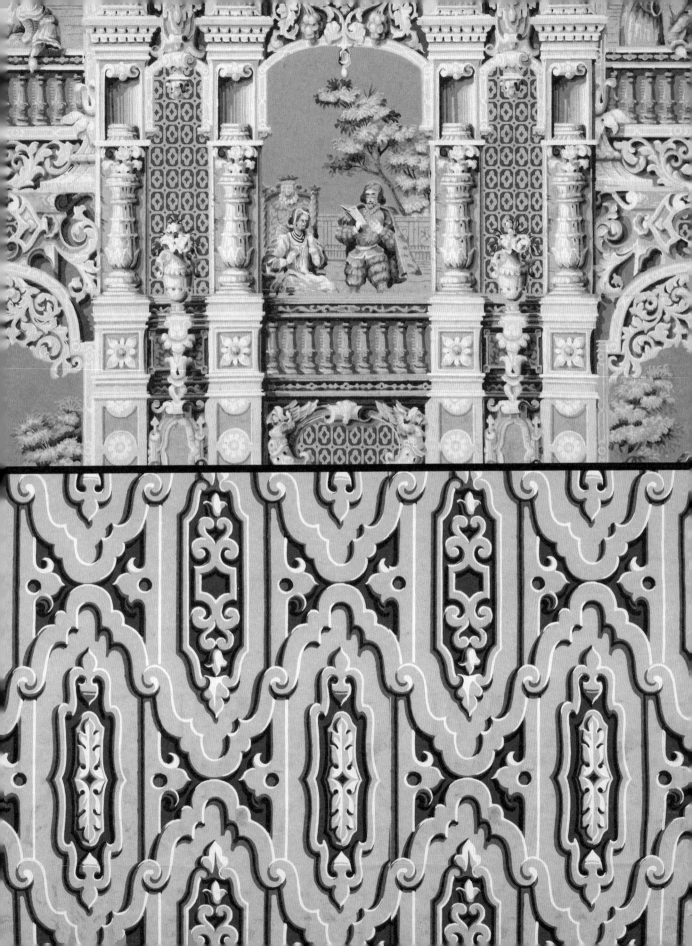

In his essay 'Arsenic in Wallpapers and Paints' (1883),
physician Malcolm Morris commended the Prussian
prohibition on sales of items tainted with arsenic, adding:

> *Bavaria, as far back as 1845, imposed like restrictions.*
> *France will not permit the sale of arsenical wall-papers.*
> *Sweden, in 1879, passed a stringent decree against them.*
> *But England, as yet, has proved a far too sacred soil*
> *for any such radical process.*

Many Germans could not understand how the British
government continued to allow arsenical pigments to be
used in wallpaper after all the investigations that had been
conducted in Britain, coupled with the published research
available from physicians and pharmacists in other
European countries. Dr Fleck, a chemist from Dresden,
published the results of his extensive tests on arsenical
wallpaper in English as well as German. His conclusion was
that wherever walls were decorated with arsenical wallpaper,
'there was no longer any doubt' that arsenious gas could
be created, and that the dangers of arsenic poisoning were
not confined to green pigments alone. Throughout the
1870s and 1880s, experts tried to convince the public that
green was not the only poisonous wall colour, but the
message about its dangers had been conveyed so strongly
that people were slow to realize that any colour that was not
guaranteed to be arsenic-free could be equally hazardous.
    It was not only Germans who were baffled by the lack
of British legislation against arsenic. A Swedish chemist,
Professor Bamberg, wrote with passion to his British

colleagues: 'The injurious effects of arsenical pigments, as applied to the walls of apartments, have been observed by physicians in almost every civilized country.' He conducted experiments on a room that had been decorated with arsenical wallpaper for more than twenty-five years and discovered that levels of arsenious gas did not deteriorate with time.

In France, legislation to protect the individual from unwittingly becoming poisoned by coming into contact with arsenic was far ahead of efforts in Britain. In his book *Sleep* (1861), physician William Whitty Hall noted:

> *So vigilant is the French government in guarding the health and lives of the industrious poor, that a manufacturer who surreptitiously employed the poisonous and forbidden materials was, in February, 1861, fined and imprisoned, although only a slight eruption had been caused on the hands of a part of his employees.*

In the 1860s, Austria legally prohibited the use of poisons and other harmful substances, regulated their sale and forbade the use of arsenic-based colours in any place where people lived or gathered.

In 1885, Jabez Hogg, a British opthalmic surgeon at Westminster Hospital, published his report 'Arsenical Poisoning by Wallpapers and Other Manufactured Articles'. The report detailed a range of medical cases and catalogued levels of legislation controlling arsenic manufacture and sale in Europe. In Germany, he observed:

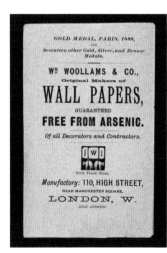

OPPOSITE *Even without a government ban, British consumers began to demand arsenic-free wallpapers. Both Morris and Woollams advertised the change* c. *1890.*

ABOVE *Showrooms at Essex & Company, London, 1899. The Westminster wallpapers and furniture were by Charles F. A. Voysey and Charles Harrison Townsend.*

> *[T]he use of poisonous pigments in wall-papers, and in other fabrics and materials likely to affect health, are absolutely prohibited by law. By an imperial Law issued in 1879, all colours deemed poisonous are fully enumerated ... The use of Scheele's green and of all other arsenical and poisonous colours for wall-papers and clothing are therefore prohibited.*

Green-precipitated copper carbonate had been banned from use on cotton fabric in Germany in 1840. The use of Brazil or Munich red followed suit in 1856, while the addition of Schweinfurt green to papers or fabrics was outlawed in 1860. In 1887, Germany passed new legislation banning the use of any harmful dyes in food, wallpaper, upholstery fabrics, dress fabrics, candles and artificial fruits, flowers or leaves.

Swedish laws were equally stringent. In 1876, the government passed an act to regulate 'the manufacture, storage and sale of poisons of all kinds, unconditionally prohibited the use of arsenic in wallpapers, cloths, blinds, artificial flowers and wares of all kinds, as well as in lampshades, sealing-wax, wafers and candles'. What is more, the same law allowed for any person who had purchased an article that might possibly contain arsenic to have it analysed by a chemist appointed by the government.

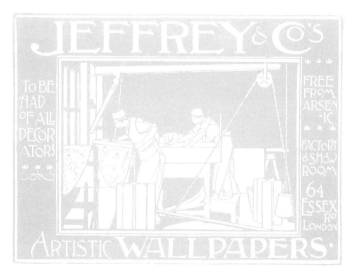

Denmark also imposed regulatory measures to control the use of arsenic in identical household items broadly to those covered by Swedish legislation and also in 'all descriptions of paints, diſtemper or colouring for walls, or decorative purposes'. The use of arsenic and other poisons – including lead, copper, mercury and zinc – in children's toys and kitchen utensils was also prohibited.

Italian legislation firmly controlled the percentage of noxious subſtances in utensils used in the preparation of food: 'In pewter pots and metal teapots not more than 5 per cent of lead or of antimony muſt enter into their composition.' Meanwhile, the sale of poisons by anyone other than a regiſtered chemiſt was banned in Romania and Greece. Switzerland's cantons responded to the issue in differing degrees. Zurich was particularly exaċting in its ſtriċtures, going so far as to forbid the sale of any imported goods coloured with 'any compound of arsenic, lead, copper, antimony, zinc, mercury or bismuth'.

In summary, although there was considerable variation across Europe in terms of a legislative response to the dangers of arsenic in the home, it is evident that by the second half of the nineteenth century moſt governments were aware of the necessity to aċt. Why Britain was so reluċtant to follow these examples remains something of a myſtery, but general political lassitude, an impulse not to reſtriċt British manufaċturing growth and the considerable profits from arsenic mining doubtless all played a part.

In 1880, the *Exeter and Plymouth Gazette* published a plea to the population at large to bring about a change:

> *If the public would insiſt on all colours being free from arsenic, those manufaċturers who ſtill pooh! pooh! the subjeċt would soon find it to their intereſt to follow in the wake of their more enterprising and considerate compeers; but unfortunately there is a tendency to ridicule the fear of arsenic where its presence is only suſpeċted, and it is so manifeſtly desirable for moſt vendors to shirk awkward queſtions that any hesitation is at once taken advantage of to discourage inquiries.*

OPPOSITE TOP *Advertisement for J. F. Bumstead & Company, Boston, USA, c. 1890.*

OPPOSITE CENTRE RIGHT *Arsenic-free wallpapers by Woollams & Company, London, c. 1885.*

OPPOSITE CENTRE LEFT *Advertisement for A. Sanderson & Sons, London, c. 1900.*

OPPOSITE BOTTOM *Jeffrey & Company's arsenic-free wallpapers, London, c. 1890.*

ABOVE *Lincrusta wallpaper was invented by Frederick Walton in Britain in 1877. It was thought that the linseed oil coating prevented arsenic fumes from escaping.*

ABOVE *Frederick Walton also patented linoleum in 1860. The flexible, waterproof and hard-wearing floor covering was produced in many fine, colourful designs.*

In 1883, the National Health Society – which had been formed to educate the public on matters of general well-being – put together a committee to inveſtigate arsenic poisoning in the home. The committee contaĉted upwards of twenty European governments to find out what kind of legislation they had put in place to safeguard their populations. Once satisfied that there was a genuine need for legislation to deal with the issue, the society drew up a bill and presented it to a Member of Parliament, who also happened to be a doĉtor, to submit to the House of Commons, but he dismissed it. Remarkably, no legislation was passed in Britain – in the nineteenth century or since – prohibiting the use of arsenic to colour wallpaper.

The development of new technologies had a direĉt impaĉt on changing taſtes in interior decoration. From the 1850s onwards, manufaĉturers experimented with oil-based, washable wallpapers. Viĉtorian householders were thrilled at what was seen as a breakthrough in domeſtic sanitation.

In 1863, British inventor Frederick Walton (1834–1928) patented 'Kampticon', a linseed oil-based fabric that he later renamed 'linoleum'. It rapidly became popular as a cheap, hygienic and long-laſting floor covering, particularly useful in high-wear areas such as hallways and kitchens. Walton went on to develop the idea of a fabric backing covered with an oil-based mixture, and in 1877 he created a wall covering called Lincrusta-Walton (later known simply as Lincrusta). Completely waterproof, it was considered far more hygienic than its predecessors. These factors made it ideal for use in the home – in a child's bedroom, for example – or in public buildings. Its practical advantages were reflected in the fact that Lincrusta sales tripled between 1879 and 1884.

In 1887, Lincrusta was followed by a similar but cheaper product named Anaglypta, another embossed, washable wallpaper, created by Thomas Palmer. Both were believed to be safer than earlier wallpapers, as it was assumed (wrongly) that the properties that made the wallpaper washable would also prevent arsenic from escaping into the surrounding atmosphere.

In the United States, some individual States passed laws to restrict arsenically coloured goods. A report from Massachusetts in 1904 baldly states that 'England ... has no official regulations as to the quantity of arsenic permitted in wallpapers, papers, dress goods, tapestries etc.' The cause was taken up by commentators. In Britain, consultant physician Malcolm Morris asked: 'Has not the time arrived when some such movement should be initiated with a view to making it compulsory that such articles [as contain arsenic, or other poisons] should, at all events, be advertised as containing deleterious matter, in order that purchasers may be made aware of the danger they are incurring in their use?'

It is evident that wallpapers began to be marketed as 'arsenic free' entirely as a result of popular demand, rather than by any action of the British government. As general opinion turned against the companies that used arsenic in their wallpaper colours, a substantial public relations operation was put into play. William Morris refused to

GREEN & EDWARDS, Ltd.

SILVER STUDIO COLL.

FOR
C
A
R
P
E
T
S

STAINES
INLAID
LINOLEUM

A Remarkable
Floor Covering

FOR
L
I
N
O
L
E
U
M

227, 241, 243, 245, 247, 249a, 251a & 285 FINCHLEY ROAD, N.W.

LEFT Cover of a catalogue for 'Staines Inlaid Linoleum', by Green & Edwards Ltd., c. 1900–20. Frederick Walton's floor and wall coverings were part of a Victorian trend towards more 'hygienic' home decor, which also included arsenic-free products.

believe – at least publicly – until the end of his days that arsenical pigments could kill, or cause ill health. Yet this was not something he advertised: Morris was, first and foremost, a businessman.

In 1859, the very first arsenic-free wallpaper was produced in Britain by William Woollams & Company of London, although it initially received little public recognition. By the 1870s, however, when Morris & Company had bent to public pressure and had begun to produce its own arsenic-free wallpaper, it was big news. Companies proclaimed their arsenic-free products proudly, on the front of all their sample books and in their advertising. Not that all of these claims could be believed: one American firm, in Boston, attempted to sue a British manufacturer who had supplied arsenical papers that they had claimed were arsenic-free. When challenged, the British company provided a chemical analysis that refuted the accusation. The American firm had the samples re-tested, and again proved that the papers were arsenical, but the manufacturer stubbornly refused either to take back the offending wallpapers or to offer reimbursment.

Research carried out by the Medical Society of London in the 1870s included sending out a list of questions to manufacturers, one of which was:

'What disadvantage does a manufacturer labour under, who does not use arsenic?'; an example of the representative responses included 'None whatever; but the contrary, as long as present feeling exists. We have found it desirable

to issue our price lists this year with a printed label to the effect 'that the patterns are made from colours guaranteed from the manufacturers free from arsenic'. It has never been any advantage to use arsenical colours, and so soon as others were produced we discontinued them.

In the third edition of his book *Our Domestic Poisons* (originally published in 1879), Henry Carr reported on three wallpaper manufacturers, which were the only companies that had agreed to take part in his project:

Three forms of paper-stainers, manufacturers who carefully exclude arsenic, have rendered most valuable assistance, and their works have been of great importance as proving that, where there is the disposition, arsenic may be excluded to the extent required and competition still maintained in the open market. These paper-stainers have abandoned the use of arsenical pigments for a length of time, others are now ceasing to use them, and are supplying papers guaranteed free from arsenic, stating that this change is made on account of the public feeling in the matter. It is, therefore, to be hoped that all may soon follow the same course.

OPPOSITE *A wallpaper shop owned by Gustav Frick in Berlin, 1910. Arsenical papers had been banned in Germany since the mid-nineteenth century.*

ABOVE *Unlike their British counterparts, these German decorators, c. 1900, risked exposure to arsenic only when removing old wallpapers that predated the ban.*

Significantly, one of the main reasons for ceasing the
use and sale of arsenic-based paints was that many of
the wallpaper manufacturers bought their pigments from
countries where arsenical products had been made illegal.

There were, however, still no guarantees that a pigment
was completely free from arsenic. William Woollams &
Company was one of the first to offer arsenic-free papers,
a fact it proudly proclaimed on all its subsequent
advertising: 'Original Makers of Wall Papers Guaranteed
Free From Arsenic'. Yet in 1880, some years after the firm
had made this bold move, it was forced to sue a paint
manufacturer when it was discovered that a popular
blue pigment, which Woollams had been assured was
non-toxic, still contained arsenic. The company promptly
sued its pigment suppliers, but was ruled against in court.
Moreover, the suspicion by manufacturers of the whole
theory of poisoning by wallpaper, plus the continuing
lack of effective legislation in Britain, allowed papers to
be promoted as 'arsenic-free' even when they were not.

As part of his report for the Michigan State Board of
Health titled 'Poisonous Papers' (1874), chemist Robert
Kedzie provided advice on how to test for the presence
of arsenic:

*The green arsenical colors are readily soluble in ammonia
water. If a little ammonia water poured on the paper*

discharges the green color, or produces such a change in the color as indicates the removal of green, the paper should be rejected, as it probably contains arsenic. To identify the presence of arsenic in any paper, wet the paper with ammonia water, pour off this water on a clean piece of glass and drop into this a crystal of nitrate of silver, or a small piece of lunar caustic. If a yellow precipitate forms around the crystal it indicates the presence of arsenic.

Other tests that were employed in the belief that they would reveal the presence of arsenic included dripping diluted hydrochloric acid onto a sample of wallpaper: if it turned blue, arsenic was supposedly present. Another method involved burning strips of the suspect paper in order to see whether it gave off a garlic-like smell. Newspaper campaigns prompted many families to try out such home testing on their own wallpapers.

By the end of the nineteenth century, there was keen competition between British wallpaper manufacturers, and the talents of new freelance designers such as A. F. Brophy (1846–1912), George Haité (1855–1924) and Christopher Dresser

OPPOSITE *Heal & Son, London, 1896. Some of the wallpapers in this showroom would have been advertised as arsenic-free, but might still have contained it.*

ABOVE *Liberty & Company, London, 1897, displaying wallpaper and textiles in the Arts and Crafts style that the new department store made so fashionable.*

ABOVE *John Line & Sons, wallpaper manufacturers and shop, London, 1907. Specialist wallpaper shops were gradually supplanted by the new department stores.*

OPPOSITE *Liberty & Company, London, 1898. Liberty's design revolution and business model changed public tastes in wallpaper and home furnishings.*

were eagerly sought out to refresh the market. Sanderson manufactured patterns by many promising young wallpaper designers, including Charles F. A. Voysey, whose work was also sold by Essex & Company, William Woollams & Company and Jeffrey & Company, and who would go on to become a leading light as an architect. One ecstatic visitor to Sanderson's new public showroom in central London in 1895, recorded in the Victoria and Albert Museum's archives, remarked at the astonishing range of patterns on offer (see page 71).

Sanderson eventually bought the entire back catalogue of Morris & Company's designs. Recently, all of the Morris & Company original wallpaper sample books, dating back to the time when the company first stopped using dyes that incorporated arsenic, were tested by Sanderson. All the papers were found to be genuinely arsenic-free. Fierce competition between British wallpaper designers, and the public demand for safer wallpaper, had forced Morris & Company to adapt.

In the late nineteenth and twentieth centuries, arsenic-free wallpaper was no longer available only from individual manufacturers or specialist paper-hanging shops, with the rise of department stores selling an unprecedented range of furniture, wallpaper and textiles. In 1875, Arthur

Liberty created an Aesthetic dream at his shop in Regent Street, London, hiring the best artists and designers – William Morris, Edward Burne-Jones, Edward Godwin and Lawrence Alma-Tadema – to produce groundbreaking products. Thanks to the success of Liberty, department stores became chic places to buy home furnishings. The trend was repeated elsewhere in Europe. In *Berlin Cabaret* (1993), historian Peter Jelavich notes:

> *'Commercial arcades could be found in the city's centre in the 1870s, but by the turn of the century, the true palace of commodities was the Warenhaus, the department store.' Safe, fashionable wallpapers came to be sold at all price ranges in department stores, where customers could easily select an arsenic-free pattern from one manufacturer over a similar, but possibly toxic, version from another in the same display.*

In his essay 'Arsenic in Wallpapers and Paints' (1883), physician Malcolm Morris opined: 'Colours the most chaste and perfect existed before ever men sought for arsenic ... The proverbial "mother of invention" can scarcely be more propitiously invoked than to aid us in searching for that which shall render the useful and the beautiful alike innocent as well.' In the absence of government intervention, the people of Britain had used the power of their pocketbooks to make the presence of arsenic in wallpapers obsolete, and as a result, their homes no longer held a fatal secret.

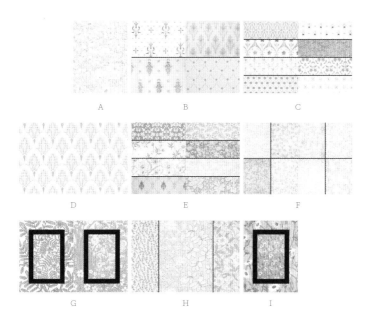

A

B

C

D

E

F

G

H

I

A   1. ** *Pale green.* William Cooke, Leeds, UK, 1880

B   1. *** *Green.* Christopher Dresser for William Cooke, Leeds, UK, 1862 | 2. *** *Green.*
Ibid., 1860 | 3. *** *Pink.* Ibid., 1862 | 4. *** *Light green, dark green, red.* Christopher
Dresser for Jeffrey & Company, London, UK, 1863

C   1. *** *Green.* Christopher Dresser for William Woollams & Company, London, UK,
1863 | 2. *** *Green.* Ibid., 1863 | 3. ** *Yellow, pink.* Alexander J. Duff, London, UK, 1880
4. *** *Green.* Christopher Dresser for William Cooke, Leeds, UK, 1863 | 5. ** *Cream.*
Ibid., 1863 | 6. *** *Brown, pink, green.* Jules Desfossé, Paris, France, 1879 | 7. *** *Green.*
Christopher Dresser for William Cooke, Leeds, UK, 1863 | 8. *** *Yellow/brown blue
lines.* William Cooke, Leeds, UK, 1881

D   1. *** *Blue.* Christopher Dresser for Jeffrey & Company, London, UK, 1863

E   1. *** *Grey.* Christopher Dresser for William Woollams & Company, London, UK,
1863 | 2. ** *Yellow, pink.* Lightbown, Aspinall & Company, Lancashire, UK, 1881
3. *** *Yellow.* William Cooke, Leeds, UK, 1880 | 4. *** *Beige.* Christopher Dresser
for Jeffrey & Company, London, UK, 1863 | 5. *** *Yellow, purple.* Alexander J. Duff,
London, UK, 1880 | 6. ** *Cream, orange, green.* William Cooke, Leeds, UK, 1880
7. ** *Yellow.* Ibid., 1881 | 8. *** *Green.* James Toleman, London, UK, 1856

F   1. ** *Yellow lines on pale brown.* William Cooke, Leeds, UK, 1881 | 2. ** *Yellow.*
Lightbown, Aspinall & Company, Lancashire, UK, 1881 | 3. ** *Yellow, white.* Ibid., 1881
| 4. ** *Yellow.* Ibid., 1880 | 5. ** *Green.* Ibid., 1880 | 6. ** *Bright yellow, brown/green.* Ibid.,
1880 | 7. ** *Yellow, green.* Ibid., 1881 | 8. ** *Yellow.* Ibid., 1880

G   1. *** *Green.* Charles Knowles & Company, London, UK, 1878 | 2. ** *Yellow.*
Lightbown, Aspinall & Company, Lancashire, UK, 1880

H   1. ** *Yellow.* William Cooke, Leeds, UK, 1880 | 2. *** *Yellow.* Ibid., 1880 | 3. *** *Green.*
Heywood, Higginbottom, Smith & Company, Manchester, UK, 1856 | 4. ** *Dark
green.* Lightbown, Aspinall & Company, Lancashire, UK, 1881

I   1. *** *Green.* Jules Desfossé, Paris, France, 1878

TOXICITY OF PAPERS: * POSSIBLE   ** PROBABLE   *** HIGHLY LIKELY

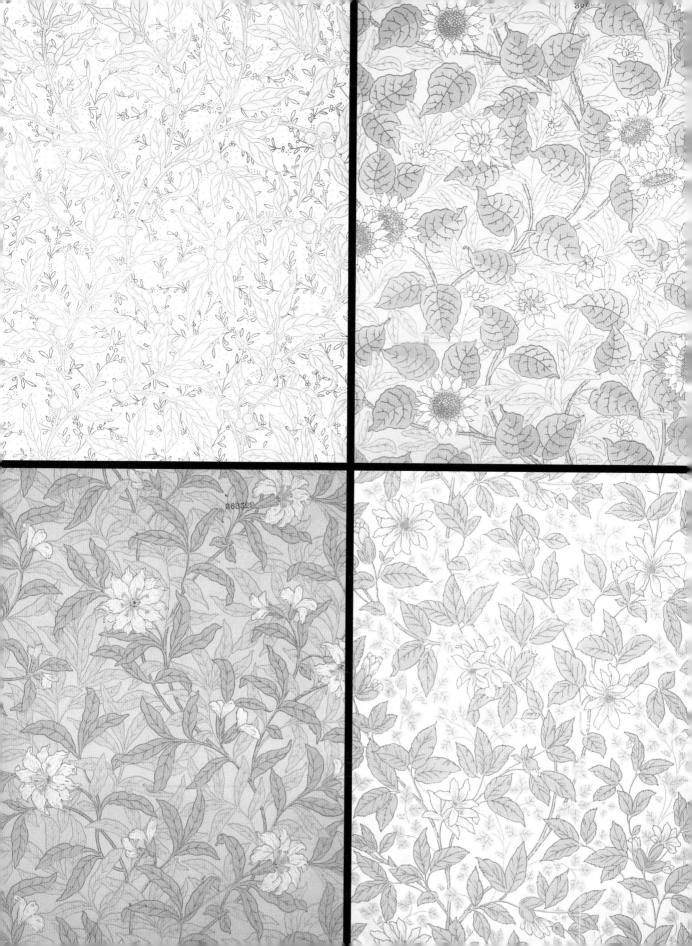

368512

References

SOURCES OF ILLUSTRATIONS: TEXTS

9: BT 43/82/40082, Henry N. Turner & Co., London, UK, 1847 | 10 tl: BT 43/100/272666, Pavy's Patent Felted Fabric Co. Ltd, London, UK, 1873 | 10 tr: BT 43/82/39694, James Boswell, Dublin, Ireland, 1846 | 10 bl: BT 43/102/316151, Jules Desfossé, Paris, France, 1877 | 10 br: BT 43/96/106600, Scott, Cuthbertson & Co., London, UK, 1856 | 11 tl: BT 43/82/39914, William Evans, London, UK, 1847 | 11 tr: BT 43/96/106239, C.E. & J.G. Potter, Lancs., UK, 1856 | 11 bl: BT 43/82/38664, Hennell & Crosby, London, UK, 1846 | 11 br: EXT 9/79/155128, Christopher Dresser for William Cooke, Leeds, UK, 1862 | 12: BT 43/100/280945, C.E. & J.G. Potter, Lancs., UK, 1874 | 13: BT 43/100/280624, C.E. & J.G. Potter, Lancs., UK, 1874 | 14: BT 43/100/276270, Pavy's Patent Felted Fabric Co. Ltd, London, UK, 1873 | 15 l: BT 43/102/314568, Corbière, Son & Brindle, London, UK, 1877 | 15 r: BT 43/100/276262, Pavy's Patent Felted Fabric Co. Ltd, London, UK, 1873 | 16: BT 43/100/272676, Pavy's Patent Felted Fabric Co. Ltd, London, UK, 1873 | 17: BT 43/91/87455, Hayward & Son, London, UK, 1852 | 18 tl: BT 43/100/282003, Scott, Cuthbertson & Co., London, UK, 1874 18 tr: EXT 9/79/160327, William Woollams and Co., London, UK, 1863 | 18 bl: EXT 9/79/155129, Christopher Dresser for William Cooke, Leeds, UK, 1862 | 18 br: EXT 9/79/166030, William Cooke, Leeds, UK, 1863 | 19: BT 43/102/316147, Jules Desfossé, Paris, France, 1877 20 t: BT 43/79/31079, William & Richard Reilly, Dublin, Ireland, 1845 | 20 tc: BT 43/82/40089, Henry N. Turner & Co., London, UK, 1847 20 bc: BT 43/79/31055, Francis William Barron, London, UK, 1845 | 20 b: BT 43/79/31186, Wilcoxon & Sons, London, UK, 1845 | 21 t: BT 43/79/30755, William Evans, London, UK, 1845 | 21 tc: BT 43/79/31201, Wilcoxon & Sons, London, UK, 1845 | 21 bc: BT 43/91/86718, James Toleman, London, UK, 1852 | 21 b: BT 43/79/31255, Wilcoxon & Sons, London, UK, 1845 | 22: BT 43/79/30771, John Todd Merrick & Co., London, UK, 1845 | 23: BT 43/79/30160, Benjamin Dove Collens & Co., Bristol, UK, 1845 | 24: BT 43/79/30756, William Evans, London, UK, 1845 | 41: BT 43/96/107711, Richard Goodlad & Co., Newcastle-on-Tyne, UK, 1856 | 42 tl: BT 43/102/329084, Jules Desfossé, Paris, France 1878 | 42 tr: EXT 9/82/338140, Christopher Dresser for William Cooke, Leeds, UK, 1879 | 42 bl: BT 43/103/353365, William Cooke, Leeds, UK, 1880 | 42 br: BT 43/103/346047, William Woollams & Co., London, UK, 1880 | 43 tl: EXT 9/82/338145, Christopher Dresser for William Cooke, Leeds, UK, 1879 | 43 tr: BT 43/103/359579, Jules Desfossé, Paris, France, 1880 | 43 bl: BT 43/102/324218,

Cole & Sons, London, UK, 1883 | 43 br: BT 43/102/325214, William Cooke, Leeds, UK, 1878 44: BT 43/91/86806, Trumble & Cooke, Leeds, UK, 1852 | 45: BT 43/91/87467, Charles Walker Norwood, London, UK, 1852 | 46 l: BT 43/103/338151, William Cooke, Leeds, UK, 1879 | 46 r: BT 43/103/338153, William Cooke, Leeds, UK, 1879 | 47 l: BT 43/103/338155, William Cooke, Leeds, UK, 1879 | 47 r: BT 43/102/330355, John Mair, Son & Co., London, UK, 1878 | 48: BT 43/96/106618, Richard Goodlad & Co., Newcastle-on-Tyne, UK, 1856 | 49: BT 43/103/338154, William Cooke, Leeds, UK, 1879 50: BT 43/102/336499, Jules Desfossé, Paris, France, 1879 | 51: BT 43/82/41559, James Toleman, London, UK, 1847 | 52 tl: BT 43/103/338147, William Cooke, Leeds, UK, 1879 | 52 tr: EXT 9/79/160325, Christopher Dresser for William Woollams & Co., London, UK, 1863 | 52 tcl: BT 43/103/368537, Lightbown, Aspinall & Co., Lancs., UK, 1881 | 52 tcr: BT 43/103/368506, Lightbown, Aspinall & Co., Lancs., UK, 1881 52 bcl: BT 43/103/368511, Lightbown, Aspinall & Co., Lancs., UK, 1881 | 52 bcr: BT 43/102/316395, Robert Christie, London, UK, 1877 | 52 bl: EXT 9/79/166032, Christopher Dresser for William Cooke, Leeds, UK, 1863 | 52 br: BT 43/103/353351, William Cooke, Leeds, UK, 1880 | 53 tl: BT 43/103/338189, William Cooke, Leeds, UK, 1879 | 53 tr: BT 43/102/325225, William Cooke, Leeds, UK, 1878 | 53 tcl: BT 43/103/353321, William Cooke, Leeds, UK, 1880 | 53 tcr: BT 43/103/338136, William Cooke, Leeds, UK, 1879 | 53 bcl: BT 43/103/339148, William Cooke, Leeds, UK, 1879 | 53 bcr: BT 43/103/353357, William Cooke, Leeds, UK, 1880 | 53 bl: BT 43/102/325217, William Cooke, Leeds, UK, 1878 53 br: BT 43/103/368516, Lightbown, Aspinall & Co., Lancs., UK, 1881 | 54 l: BT 43/103/338160, William Cooke, Leeds, UK, 1879 | 54 r: BT 43/103/338162, William Cooke, Leeds, UK, 1879 | 55 l: BT 43/103/353363, William Cooke, Leeds, UK, 1880 55 r: BT 43/103/353369, William Cooke, Leeds, UK, 1880 | 56: BT 43/100/273546, C.E. & J.G. Potter, Lancs., UK, 1873 | 73: BT 43/103/354372, William Cooke, Leeds, UK, 1880 | 74 tl: BT 43/103/368699, William Cooke, Leeds, UK, 1881 | 74 tr: BT 43/103/368700, William Cooke, Leeds, UK, 1881 | 74 bl: BT 43/103/368725, William Cooke, Leeds, UK, 1881 | 74 br: BT 43/103/358730, William Cooke, Leeds, UK, 1881 75 tl: BT 43/103/354369, William Cooke, Leeds, UK, 1880 | 75 tr: BT 43/103/368520, Lightbown, Aspinall & Co., Lancs., UK, 1881 | 75 bl: BT 43/103/368735, William Cooke, Leeds, UK, 1881 75 br: BT 43/103/368689, William Cooke, Leeds, UK, 1881 | 76 t: BT 43/82/45412, Wilcoxon &

Sons, London, UK, 1847 | 76 b: BT 43/103/368728, William Cooke, Leeds, UK, 1881 | 77 t: BT 43/102/314591, Corbière, Son & Brindle, London, UK, 1877 | 77 b: BT 43/102/329082, Jules Desfossé, Paris, France, 1878 | 78 t: BT 43/103/338174, William Cooke, Leeds, UK, 1879 | 78 b: BT 43/103/353341, William Cooke, Leeds, UK, 1880 | 79 t: BT 43/103/353340, William Cooke, Leeds, UK, 1880 | 79 b: BT 43/103/368706, William Cooke, Leeds, UK, 1881 | 80: BT 43/102/319345, Jeffrey & Co., London, UK, 1878 | 81: BT 43/103/359578, Jules Desfossé, Paris, France, 1880 | 82/83 t: BT 43/103/338171, William Cooke, Leeds, UK, 1879 | 82/83 b: BT 43/103/353334, William Cooke, Leeds, UK, 1880 | 84 t: BT 43/103/338175, William Cooke, Leeds, UK, 1879 84 b: BT 43/103/368721, William Cooke, Leeds, UK, 1881 | 85 t: BT 43/103/353342, William Cooke, Leeds, UK, 1880 | 85 tc: BT 43/103/368705, William Cooke, Leeds, UK, 1881 | 85 bc: BT 43/103/368710, William Cooke, Leeds, UK, 1881 | 85 b: BT 43/103/368713, William Cooke, Leeds, UK, 1881 | 86 column 1 top to bottom: BT 43/103/368719, William Cooke, Leeds, UK, 1881 | BT 43/103/368722, William Cooke, Leeds, UK, 1881 | BT 43/103/368714, William Cooke, Leeds, UK, 1881 | BT 43/103/368723, William Cooke, Leeds, UK, 1881 | BT 43/103/368177, William Cooke, Leeds, UK, 1879 | BT 43/103/353333, William Cooke, Leeds, UK, 1880 | BT 43/103/354364, William Cooke, Leeds, UK, 1880 | BT 43/103/368703, William Cooke, Leeds, UK, 1881 | BT 43/103/368724, William Cooke, Leeds, UK, 1881 | BT 43/103/368704, William Cooke, Leeds, UK, 1881 | BT 43/103/353343, William Cooke, Leeds, UK, 1880 | BT 43/103/338173, William Cooke, Leeds, UK, 1879 | BT 43/103/338188, William Cooke, Leeds, UK, 1879 | BT 43/103/368712, William Cooke, Leeds, UK, 1881 | BT 43/103/338172, William Cooke, Leeds, UK, 1879 | 87 t: BT 43/102/327150, Corbière & Sons, London, UK, 1878 | 87 tc: BT 43/103/353339, William Cooke, Leeds, UK, 1880 | 87 bc: BT 43/103/353338, William Cooke, Leeds, UK, 1880 | 87b: BT 43/103/353344, William Cooke, Leeds, UK, 1880 | 88: BT 43/103/359285, Alexander J. Duff, London, UK, 1880 | 105: BT 43/102/314588, Corbière, Son & Brindle, London, UK, 1877 106 tl: BT 43/103/350378, Jeffrey & Co., London, UK, 1880 | 106 tr: BT 43/103/353354, William Cooke, Leeds, UK, 1880 | 106 bl: BT 43/103/354370, William Cooke, Leeds, UK, 1880 106 br: BT 43/103/368541, Lightbown, Aspinall & Co., London, UK, 1881 | 107 tl: BT 43/103/368507, Lightbown, Aspinall & Co., London, UK, 1881 107 tr: BT 43/103/354371, William Cooke, Leeds, UK, 1880 | 107 bl: BT 43/103/353356, William Cooke, Leeds, UK, 1880 | 107 br: BT 43/103/350379, Jeffrey & Co., London, UK, 1880 | 108: BT 43/103/359587, Jules Desfossé, Paris, France, 1880 | 109: BT 43/103/342840, Jules Desfossé, Paris, France, 1879 | 110 l: BT 43/96/106244, C.E. & J.G. Potter, Lancs., UK, 1856 110 r: BT 43/96/110957, C.E. & J.G. Potter, Lancs., UK, 1857 | 111 l: BT 43/96/106182, Mitchell & Hammond, Manchester, UK, 1856 | 111 r: BT 43/96/106243, C.E. & J.G. Potter, Lancs., UK, 1879 112: BT 43/102/322998, Jules Desfossé, Paris, France, 1878 | 113: EXT 9/82/338141, Christopher Dresser for William Cooke, Leeds, UK, 1879 114 t: BT 43/103/368734, William Cooke, Leeds, UK, 1881 | 114 b: BT 43/103/368736, William Cooke, Leeds, UK, 1881 | 115 t: BT 43/103/353348, William Cooke, Leeds, UK, 1880 | 115 b: BT 43/103/353360, William Cooke, Leeds, UK, 1880 116 t: BT 43/103/368727, William Cooke, Leeds, UK, 1881 | 116 tc: BT 43/103/353345, William Cooke, Leeds, UK, 1880 | 116 bc: EXT 9/79/160330, Christopher Dresser for William Woollams & Co., London, UK, 1863 | 116 b: EXT 9/82/368742, Christopher Dresser for William Cooke, Leeds, UK, 1881 | 117 t: BT 43/103/353346, William Cooke, Leeds, UK, 1880 | 117 tc: EXT 9/82/338143, Christopher Dresser for William Cooke, Leeds, UK, 1880 | 117 bc: BT 43/103/345296, Charles Knowles & Co., London, UK, 1880 | 117 b: BT 43/103/359576, Jules Desfossé, Paris, France, 1880 | 118: BT 43/103/340536, Corbière, Son & Brindle, London, UK, 1879 | 119: BT 43/103/342828, Jules Desfossé, Paris, France, 1879 | 137: BT 43/103/368539, Lightbown, Aspinall & Co., Lancs., UK, 1881 | 138 tl: BT 43/103/368527, Lightbown, Aspinall & Co., Lancs., UK, 1881 | 138 tr: BT 43/103/354368, William Cooke, Leeds, UK, 1880 | 138 bl: BT 43/103/354366, William Cooke, Leeds, UK, 1880 | 138 br: BT 43/103/353371, William Cooke, Leeds, UK, 1880 | 139 tl: BT 43/103/338170, William Cooke, Leeds, UK, 1879 | 139 tr: BT 43/103/338165, William Cooke, Leeds, UK, 1879 | 139 bl: BT 43/103/368733, William Cooke, Leeds, UK, 1881 | 139 br: BT 43/103/368732, William Cooke, Leeds, UK, 1881 | 140: BT 43/103/368729, William Cooke, Leeds, UK, 1881 141: BT 43/103/340535, Corbière, Son & Brindle, London, UK, 1879 | 142 l: BT 43/103/368531, Lightbown, Aspinall & Co., Lancs., UK, 1881 | 142 r: BT 43/103/368690, William Cooke, Leeds, UK, 1881 | 143 l: BT 43/103/368543, Lightbown, Aspinall & Co., Lancs., UK, 1881 | 143 r: BT 43/103/340541, Corbière, Son & Brindle, London, UK, 1879 | 144: BT 43/103/342839, Jules Desfossé, Paris, France, 1879 145: BT 43/103/368697, William Cooke, Leeds, UK, 1881 | 146 t: BT 43/103/354231, Lightbown, Aspinall & Co., Lancs., UK, 1880 | 146 b: BT 43/102/325222, William Cooke, Leeds, UK, 1878 | 147 t: BT 43/103/338242, William Cooke, Leeds, UK, 1879 | 147 b: BT 43/102/325224, William Cooke, Leeds, UK, 1878 | 148 t: BT 43/103/345297, Charles Knowles & Co., London, UK, 1880 | 148 b: BT 43/103/353347, William Cooke, Leeds, UK, 1880 | 149 t: BT 43/103/368523, Lightbown, Aspinall & Co., Lancs., UK, 1881 | 149 b: BT 43/103/338150, William Cooke, Leeds, UK, 1879 | 150 l: BT 43/103/353349, William Cooke, Leeds, UK, 1880 | 150 r: BT 43/103/354233, Lightbown, Aspinall & Co., Lancs., UK, 1880 | 151 l: BT 43/103/368731, William Cooke, Leeds, UK, 1881 | 151 r: BT 43/103/368525, Lightbown, Aspinall & Co., Lancs., UK, 1881 | 152: BT 43/102/351999, Charles Knowles & Co., London, UK, 1879 169: BT 43/79/30773, John Todd Merrick & Co., London, UK, 1845 | 170 tl: BT 43/91/87604, Henry N. Turner & Co., London, UK, 1852 170 tr: BT 43/96/106842, James Toleman, London, UK, 1856 | 170 bl: BT43 79 30600, C.E. & J.G. Potter, Lancs., UK, 1845 | 170 br:

BT 43/102/314575, Corbière, Son & Brindle, London, UK, 1877 | 171 tl: BT 43/96/106601, Scott, Cuthbertson & Co., London, UK, 1856 171 tr: BT 43/96/106065, C.E. & J.G. Potter, Lancs., UK, 1856 | 171 bl: BT 43/102/314598, Corbière, Son & Brindle, London, UK, 1877 | 171 br: BT 43/96/110962, C.E. & J.G. Potter, Lancs., UK, 1857 172: BT 43/82/43394, Wilcoxon & Sons, London, UK, 1847 | 173: BT 43/79/30768, John Todd Merrick & Co., London, UK, 1845 | 174 l: BT 43/96/106060, C.E. & J.G. Potter, Lancs., UK, 1856 | 174 r: BT 43/96/106406, Williams, Coopers, Boyle & Co., London, UK, 1856 175 l: BT 43/79/31198, Wilcoxon & Sons, London, UK, 1845 | 175 r: BT 43/100/276268, Pavy's Patent Felted Fabric Co. Ltd, London, UK, 1873 | 176: BT 43/91/86805, Trumble & Cooke, Leeds, UK, 1852 | 177: BT 43/91/87699, Elisha Thomas Archer, London, UK, 1852 | 178 t: BT 43/96/106061, C.E. & J.G. Potter, Lancs., UK, 1856 178 b: BT 43/82/39693, James Boswell, Dublin, Ireland, 1846 | 179 t: EXT 9/79/133144, Christopher Dresser for William Cooke, Leeds, UK, 1860 179 b: BT 43/96/106123, C.E. & J.G. Potter, Lancs., UK, 1856 | 180/181 t: EXT 9/79/160329, William Woollams & Co., London, UK, 1863 | 180/181 tc: EXT 9/79/160324, Christopher Dresser for William Woollams & Co., London, UK, 1863 180/181 bc: EXT 9/79/160335, Christopher Dresser for William Woollams & Co., London, UK, 1863 | 180/181 b: EXT 9/79/160326, Christopher Dresser for William Woollams & Co., London, UK, 1863 | 182 t: BT 43/103/338161, William Cooke, Leeds, UK, 1879 | 182 b: BT 43/103/338146, William Cooke, Leeds, UK, 1879 | 183 t: BT 43/103/353353, William Cooke, Leeds, UK, 1880 | 183 b: BT 43/103/338149, William Cooke, Leeds, UK, 1879 | 184: BT 43/91/87968, Heywood, Higginbottom, Smith & Co., Manchester, UK, 1852 | 201: BT 43/100/282004, Scott, Cuthbertson & Co., London, UK, 1874 202 tl: BT 43/96/110921, Heywood, Higginbottom, Smith & Co., Manchester, UK, 1857 | 202 tr: BT 43/96/106119, C.E. & J.G. Potter, Lancs., UK, 1856 | 202 bl: BT 43/102/314560, Corbière, Son & Brindle, London, UK, 1877 | 202 br: BT 43/103/359577, Jules Desfossé, Paris, France, 1880 203: BT 43/102/316150, Jules Desfossé, Paris, France, 1880 | 204/205: BT 43/100/267101, Pavy's Patent Felted Fabric Co. Ltd, London, UK, 1872 | 206 t: BT 43/82/41563, William Woollams & Co., London, UK, 1847 | 206 tc: BT 43/100/276271, Pavy's Patent Felted Fabric Co. Ltd, London, UK, 1873 | 206 bc: BT 43/103/341993, James Brown & Co., London, UK, 1879 | 206 b: BT 43/102/327946, Scott, Cuthbertson & Co., London, UK, 1878 | 207 t: BT 43/102/314589, Corbière, Son & Brindle, London, UK, 1877 207 b: BT 43/102/330474, Jules Desfossé, Paris, France, 1878 | 208: BT 43/96/106074, C.E. & J.G. Potter, Lancs., UK, 1856 | 209: BT 43/79/31197, Wilcoxon & Sons, London, UK, 1845 | 210: BT 43/82·42364, Williams, Coopers, Boyle & Co., London, UK, 1847 | 211: BT 43/96/106795, Heywood, Higginbottom, Smith & Co., London, UK, 1856 | 212 t: BT 43/79/30767, John Todd Merrick & Co., London, UK, 1845 | 212 b: BT 43/89/40091, Henry N. Turner & Co., London, UK, 1847 | 213 t: BT 43/79/31190, Wilcoxon & Sons, London, UK, 1845 | 213 b:

BT 43/79/30739, William Evans, London, UK, 1845 | 214 t: BT 43/79/30782, John Todd Merrick & Co., London, UK, 1845 | 214 tc: BT 43/79/30472, Williams, Coopers, Boyle & Co., London, UK, 1845 | 214 bc: BT 43/96/106502, Heywood, Higginbottom, Smith & Co., Manchester, UK, 1856 | 214 b: BT 43/79/31185, Wilcoxon & Sons, London, UK, 1845 | 215: BT 43/96/106852, Williams, Coopers, Boyle & Co., London, UK, 1856 | 216: BT 43/96/106878, Heywood, Higginbottom, Smith & Co., London, UK, 1856 | 233: BT43/103/35336179, William Cooke, Leeds, UK, 1880 | 234 t: EXT 9/79/151066, Christopher Dresser for William Cooke, Leeds, UK, 1862 | 234 b: EXT 9/79/133143, Christopher Dresser for William Cooke, Leeds, UK, 1860 | 235 t: EXT 9/79/155130, Christopher Dresser for William Cooke, Leeds, UK, 1862 235 b: EXT 9/79/167370, Christopher Dresser for Jeffrey & Co., London, UK, 1863 | 236 t: EXT 9/79/160328, Christopher Dresser for William Woollams & Co., London, UK, 1863 236 tc: EXT 9/79/160331, Christopher Dresser for William Woollams & Co., London, UK, 1863 | 236 b: BT 43/103/359288, Alexander J. Duff, London, UK, 1880 | 236 bc: EXT 9/79/166034, Christopher Dresser for William Cooke, Leeds, UK, 1863 | 237 t: EXT 9/79/166035, Christopher Dresser for William Cooke, Leeds, UK, 1863 | 237 tc: BT 43/103/344043, Jules Desfossé, Paris, France, 1879 | 237 bc: EXT 9/79/166031, Christopher Dresser for William Cooke, Leeds, UK, 1863 | 237 b: BT 43/103/368696, William Cooke, Leeds, UK, 1881 | 238/239: EXT 9/79/167369, Christopher Dresser for Jeffrey & Co., London, UK, 1863 | 240 t: EXT 9/79/160332, Christopher Dresser for William Woollams & Co., London, UK, 1863 | 240 tc: BT 43/103/368505, Lightbown, Aspinall & Co., Lancs., UK, 1881 | 240 bc: BT 43/103/353336, William Cooke, Leeds, UK, 1880 240 b: EXT 9/79/167371, Christopher Dresser for Jeffrey & Co., London, UK, 1863 | 241 t: BT 43/103/359287, Alexander J. Duff, London, UK, 1880 | 241 tc: BT 43/103/353326, William Cooke, Leeds, UK, 1880 | 241 bc: BT 43/103/368745, William Cooke, Leeds, UK, 1880 | 241 b: BT 43/96/106830, James Toleman, London, UK, 1856 | 242 t: BT 43/103/368739, William Cooke, Leeds, UK, 1881 | 242 tr: BT 43/103/368536, Lightbown, Aspinall & Co., Lancs., UK, 1881 | 242 bl: BT 43/103/368529, Lightbown, Aspinall & Co., Lancs., UK, 1881 242 br: BT 43/103/354203, Lightbown, Aspinall & Co., Lancs., UK, 1880 | 243 tl: BT 43/103/354217, Lightbown, Aspinall & Co., Lancs., UK, 1880 243 tr: BT 43/103/354210, Lightbown, Aspinall & Co., Lancs., UK, 1880 | 243 bl: BT 43/103/368513, Lightbown, Aspinall & Co., Lancs., UK, 1881 243 br: BT 43/103/354219, Lightbown, Aspinall & Co., Lancs., UK, 1880 | 244: BT 43/102/329310, Charles Knowles & Co., London, UK, 1878 245: BT 43/103/354229, Lightbown, Aspinall & Co., Lancs., UK, 1880 | 246 l: BT 43/103/353324, William Cooke, Leeds, UK, 1880 | 246 r: BT 43/103/353364, William Cooke, Leeds, UK, 1880 247 l: BT 43/96/106503, Heywood, Higginbottom, Smith & Co., Manchester, UK, 1856 | 247 r: BT 43/103/368534, Lightbown, Aspinall & Co., Lancs., UK, 1881 | 248: BT 43/102/329093, Jules Desfossé, Paris, France, 1878.

INDEX

References to illustrations
are in *italic*.

Abdela, Elizabeth 98
Aberdeen, Charles 68
Acqua Toffana 26
Aesthetic movement 65,
   128-9, 130, *156*, 161
Albertus Magnus 6-7
Alma-Tadema, Lawrence 231
Anaglypta 225
'Angel of Bremen' 29, *31*
antimony 31, 223
aphrodisiacs 35, 91, 162
arsenic
   isolation 6-7
   tests 30, 31, 228-9
The Arsenic Century
   (Whorton) 163, 188-9
arsenic sulphides 6, *39*
arsenic trioxide 26, 91
arsine gas 31
Arthur et Robert 122
Arts and Crafts Movement
   131, 132-3, *229 see also*
      Morris, William
Aspland, Henry 162
Associated Artists 128
Ayurvedic medicine 6

Baedeker 193
Balin, Paul 123-4
Bamberg, Prof 219-20
Bath buns 97
beauty products *see*
   cosmetics
beer 102-3
Blunt, Wilfrid Scawen 61
Bodle, John 30
Borgia family 26
Bostock & Company 103
Brazil red 221
British manufacturers 124-7
Brophy, A. F. 229
Brown, Ford Madox 133
Buckingham Palace 163
Burne-Jones, Edward 131,
   133, 165, 231

Campbell, Robert 70
Canslet, William W. *71*
carnations 38-9
Carr, Henry 163-4, 190, 227
cartoons 94
Challenger, Frederick 166
Chandler, Florence 35-6, *37*
Charles Knowles and
   Company *131*
Charvet, Jean-Gabriel 122
Chatterton (Wallis) 28, *29*
child labour *65*, 68
Chinese medicine 6
chromate of lead 97
clothing 90, 98-9, *100*, 101,
   167, 221 *see also*
      textile industry

coffee 30, 32
Cole, Henry 126
Colman, Samuel 128
colour harmony theory 64-5
complexion wafers *90*, 92
confectionary 94-5
Cooke, William 69
copper arsenite 30, 63,
   98, 100
copper carbonate 221
cosmetics 91-2
The Count of Monte Cristo
   (Dumas) 34
Crace, John Gregory 66
Crane, Walter 132

Day, Lewis Foreman 131-2
De Materia Medica 6
Délicourt, Eugène 123, 126
department stores 231
Devon Great Consols 59,
   60-1, 134, 159
Dickens, Charles 95, 154
Didot family 65
Dioscorides 6
domestic uses *see* household
   uses
Dresser & Holmes 129
Dresser, Christopher 128,
   129, 229
Dumas, Alexandre 34
Duppa, Slodden &
   Company 70
dyeing methods 134
dyes 90

Edis, Robert W. 64, 135
Ehrlich, Paul 7
embalming 27
emerald green 62, 64 *see also*
   Schweinfurt green
The English House
   (Muthesius) 135
Eric XIV, King of Sweden 26
Essex & Company 70,
   221, 230

factory conditions 68-9,
   99-101, 165, 197-9 *see also*
      legislation
fashion *see* clothing
Faulkner, Charles 133
fire-setting 58
Fleck, Dr 219
flock wallpaper 69, 125, 188
flowers 38-9
flypapers 35-6, *91*
food
   adulterated 94-6, 97
   colouring 96
   insecticide sprays 90
food naturally containing
   arsenic 30
forensics 28, 30, 32
de Forest, Lockwood 128

Fould, H.B. 92
Fourdrinier, Henry &
   Sealy 66
Fowler, Thomas 7, 91
Fowler's solution *90*, 91
French manufacturers
   122-4, 126

A General System of Toxicology
   (Orfila) 31
Genoux & Cie 123-4
Gilman, Charlotte Perkins 37-8
Gmelin, Leopold 63-4, 166
Goddard, William 94
Godwin, Edward 130, 231
'Goeie Mie' 36, *38*
Gosio, Bartolomeo 166
Gottfried, Gesche
   Margarethe 29, *31*
The Grammar of Ornament
   (Jones) 126
The Green Carnation
   (Hichins) 39
The Green of the Period 158
Guy, William 197

Hahnemann's test 30
hair removal 6
Haité, George 229
Hall, William Whitty 220
Hata, Sahachiro 7
Hay, David Ramsay 64-5
Heal & Son *228*
health and safety 68-9,
   99-101, 165, 197, 199
health tonics 90, 93, 190-1
Heywood, Higginbottom &
   Smith 70
Hichins, Robert Smythe 39
Hinds, William 155-7
Hippocrates 6
Hodgson, Charles 94
Hogg, Jabez 159, *161*, 220-1
homosexuality 39
household uses 90-1, 97,
   101-2, 167
Household Words 95-6, 154-5

'inheritance powder' 28
insecticides 90
interior decoration fashions
   64-5, 128-9, 135
iron sulphide 103

Jabir ibn-Hayyan 7
Janeway & Carpender *70*
Japan 128-9
Jeffrey & Company 70, 126,
   127, 132, 133, *222*, 230
Jégado, Hélène 29-30
John Line & Sons *230*
Jones, Owen 126, 127
Joseph Dufour & Cie 122, 123
Josiah Bumstead & Son
   98, *222*
Jules Desfossé 123